Contents

III

The 52 Most Romantic Dates In and Around New York City

Sheree Bykofsky

Adams Media Corporation

Avon, Massachusetts

To My Beloved New York City

Published by

Adams Media Corporation

57 Littlefield Street, Avon, MA 02322. U.S.A.

www.adamsmedia.com

ISBN: 1-58062-462-6

Printed in Canada

J I H G F E D C

Library of Congress Cataloging-in-Publication data available upon request from the publisher.

This publication is designed to provide accurate and authoritative information with regard to the subject matter covered. It is sold with the understanding that the publisher is not engaged in rendering legal, accounting, or other professional advice. If legal advice or other expert assistance is required, the services of a competent professional person should be sought.

—From a *Declaration of Principles* jointly adopted by a Committee of the American Bar Association and a Committee of Publishers and Associations

Cover illustration:

The Stock Illustration Source / ©Kalika Stern

This book is available at quantity discounts for bulk purchases. For information, call 1-800-872-5627.

$\mathcal{F}$oreword
by Arthur Schwartz

After my first trip to Venice many, many years ago, I swore I would not return until I could come back with someone I loved. Venice is too excruciatingly romantic to be visited alone. The lacy, extravagant, exotic architecture, the endless water, the gondoliers in costume, the colorfully narrow streets punctuated by surprise piazzas, the famously soft, beautifying light—to merely name some tangibles—carried me away to an emotional and spiritual place where I wanted mysterious love, excitement, adventure to exist. It was no fun alone.

Then I made a friend who grew up in Venice. At the time, he lived in New York. He hated going back. "My parents are there, my family squabbles, the water is filthy, the winter weather is so bad, the houses are poorly heated, they leak." He understood why I thought his home town was romantic beyond belief, but New York did for him what Venice did for me. Fortunately, he lived in Manhattan with someone he loved.

As a native New Yorker, it is often hard for me to see my own city as a romantic destination. Romance involves an element of surprise and I know New York too well. Or I thought I knew it too well until I read Sheree Bykofsky's book. Even places I totally take for granted, Sheree has given new dimension. She has even made going to Rockefeller Center—and there could not be a more hackneyed "romantic" spot in the city—a new experience. She has opened my eyes about restaurants I like and don't like. She's reminded me about hideaways I'd long forgotten existed. She has ferreted out places in the hinterlands that I had no idea were there. Even for me, a jaded, well-traveled New Yorker who has never been afraid of crossing a bridge, taking my car through a tunnel, or bucking traffic on one of our many suburban highways, she's provided many new excursions to enjoy with someone I love, or just friends looking for a day of discovery and adventure in our own backyard.

When listeners call me on my radio program to ask for romantic restaurant recommendations I throw the question back at them. What do you consider romantic? A quiet table in the corner? Low lighting? Candlelight? Voluptuous flower arrangements? Red rooms? Purple rooms? Is glamour synonymous with romance to you? Dancing in the dark? A post-prandial walk in the park? Must it be a room with a view? What constitutes "romantic" is so very subjective. Even so, New York and its environs has it all, plus so much more. (Well, okay, quiet tables in corners are pretty scarce.) I've always lived here. I should know. But I didn't. I look forward to following up on Sheree's discoveries. I think it is going to be like turning a street corner and suddenly laying eyes on your new love. A flutter in the chest. A flush on the face. A spasm down the back. The incomparable shiver of romance.

Acknowledgments

First and foremost, I must thank the following lovable friends for contributing entries to this book: Sharon Naylor, who puts the dance in romance; Mark Ruderman, who was often the "we" mentioned herein; Janet Rosen, who created and produced the most interesting dates for you; Chester Freeman, a true Renaissance man; Heidi Atlas, my dear friend; Maris Kreizman, Laura Goldstein, and Lisa Liebman, the best interns an agent could ever hope to have; and Paige Wheeler, my proof that competitors both win when they're friends. I would also like to thank the following people for their help and suggestions: Shaun Arnold, Elizabeth Beier, Megan Buckley, Kevin Hannan, Mitch Horowitz, Harvey Jordan, Brian Kingman, Marc Myers, Dave Ores (Dr. Dave), Larry Samuel, and all the people I met along the way. And I'll always be grateful to Steve.

I'm also indebted to my friend and editor Jere Calmes, Dawn Thompson, and to the other kind folks at Adams Media for believing in me including Gary Krebs, Laura MacLaughlin, and Kate Epstein. Thanks, too, for hiring the world's best copyeditor, Virginia Rubens.

$\mathcal{I}$ntroduction

Ever since I wrote *The Best Places to Kiss in and Around New York City*, people have asked me to name my favorite romantic place. The best I can do is tell you my 52 favorites—one for each week of the year. Because in New York City, every week brings a new definition of what is romantic. Exploring the New York City region is just like falling in love. The passion and pulse and excitement, the 24-hour possibilities, the day, the night, the sweeping cityscapes and the bucolic country scenes, the variety, the intensity, the newness, the majesty. It's the very essence of love.

It's true that if you're in love, you will find pleasure in any surroundings, and if you're completely engrossed in each other, you may not always be aware of your surroundings, anyway. But certain places have qualities that attract lovers, and if you have a romantic heart, beautiful places call out to be shared. Glorious vistas cannot be fully experienced without the right companion. Certain quiet restaurants with flowers, fireplaces, and candlelight are just meant for couples. You're likely to feel uncomfortable if you dine alone or on business in one of them. You don't want to discuss your insurance policy while that man is proposing on bended knee, do you? Similarly, if you're proposing, you don't want to be upstaged by loud suits cutting a deal.

Places that enhance love and romance in and around New York City abound. It was no easy task selecting my 52 favorites. But my romantic friends and I had fun finding the best of the best for you. We kept in mind that sometimes you would be looking for a place to dress formally and at other times you would want to unwind in shorts and sneakers. Sometimes money is no object, but alas, for most of us, usually it is. On Sunday you'll want to picnic; on Thursday you'll want to dine. One day you'll just want to immerse yourself in the city, and the next day you may need to escape. You may be seeking just the right venue to celebrate a birthday, anniversary, or other occasion. Or you may just be tired of going to the movies and watching TV together. Whatever kind of place you're seeking for a romantic day, date, or weekend, I expect you'll find it in this book. But keep in mind, this is romance from a New Yorker's point of view. People who live in the Pacific Northwest or Vermont, for example, might not find the views of nature in Central Park breathtaking, although the vibrancy of life and the mix of interesting people and sights is sure to generate warm feelings.

And the notion of what is romantic varies from person to person, day to day, season to season, occasion to occasion. One bright summer day, a picnic in the park may be just what the doctor ordered, whereas the only thing for fueling an October passion may be a country drive past the vibrant autumn foliage. A winter love may need to be stoked by the fireplace with hot chocolate, while on a fine spring day you may wake with the desire to bathe yourselves in roses at a botanical garden.

Please read the entries fully. If you're looking for an opulently elegant restaurant for a special occasion, don't select a casual one—unless that's what the two of you have agreed is the most romantic environment. The same place that will enchant you on a weeknight will not measure up for Valentine's Day or for your long-awaited marriage proposal. It has been my aim to describe the ambience of each place as completely as possible so that you can decide whether it meets your current needs. And, if money is an object, do check the prices ahead of time, as they may change frequently.

By the way, Valentine's Day presents a special challenge to lovers in New York. Ironically, some restaurants that make a random Tuesday seem like a night in heaven transform themselves into overpriced, overcrowded factories on that one night when the whole world is seeking candlelight and roses. If you use this book to help you select a Valentine's Day restaurant, please do some planning to avoid disappointment later. Call well in advance to make reservations, and ask what the restaurant's plans are for Valentine's Day. Will the regular menu be available? If not, what is the cost of the prix fixe? Will you be expected to give up your table at a certain time? Will they be changing the configurations of the tables? The same goes for New Year's Eve.

But this book is neither a comprehensive restaurant guide nor a Valentine's Day Planner. It has been my aim to find for you 52 of the most romantic places in the area—inns, parks, walks, views, hotels—places that will give you pleasure every day of the year. As far as restaurants go, I've tried to include some of the most enchanting restaurants that are not the most expensive (or at least are a good value) and ones that you may not run into in every guidebook, plus some of my favorite places to celebrate a special occasion—or even to propose. And I've also included a few restaurants that are a little less well-known for a casual date. I've provided the descriptions. It's up to you to bring the romance.

I hope you have fun together tracing some of the dates I've laid out for you, but I know you'll bring to it your own special touch. May I suggest that you use this book as the foundation to create your own collection of romantic dates. With just a little initiative, you can find a lot more to do together than just having dinner or watching TV. It's my hope that this book will inspire you to keep searching for creative things to do together and to keep your love alive wherever you happen to find yourselves.

I encourage you to be romantic adventurers. If a destination falls short of your expectations or if you get lost, chances are good you'll have a good laugh together—that is, if you make a point of enjoying the experience of being together as well as the places themselves. Just remember how lucky you are: you have each other.

$\mathscr{A}$bbracciamento on the Pier

ADDRESS: 2200 ROCKAWAY PARKWAY, BROOKLYN, NY 11236 ♥
PHONE: 718-251-5517 ♥ **HOURS:** SUNDAY THROUGH THURSDAY
11:30 A.M. TO 11:30 P.M.; FRIDAY AND SATURDAY 11:00 A.M. TO
2:30 A.M. ♥ **LIVE MUSIC HOURS:** PIANO TUESDAY, WEDNESDAY,
AND THURSDAY 7:00 TO 10:00 P.M. AND SUNDAY 12:00 TO 9:00 P.M.;
FRIDAY PIANO AND CABARET SINGER 8:00 TO 1:00 A.M.; JAZZ TRIO
SATURDAY NIGHT 8:00 TO 1:00 A.M.; BRUNCH BUFFET (NO MENU)
11:00 A.M. TO 2:30 P.M. SOMETIMES CLOSED ON SATURDAY AFTER-
NOON FOR PRIVATE PARTIES AND WEDDINGS. ♥ **DIRECTIONS:** TAKE
THE BELT PARKWAY TO EXIT 13 AND DRIVE SOUTH ON ROCKAWAY
PARKWAY STRAIGHT ONTO THE CANARSIE PIER. ♥ **PRICE:** MODERATE

Romance and Brooklyn are not incompatible when you
select a special spot. Open since 1984, Abbracciamento
on the Pier is a spacious waterside restaurant with a
graceful view of Jamaica Bay. The large window and
terrace faces west towards the Verrazano-Narrows
Bridge, and so I highly recommend making your reservations for an outdoor or window table at a time that
will allow you to maximize your enjoyment of the
sunset. It's right beside Kennedy Airport, and you'll see
the underbellies of planes coming and going—perhaps
inspiring you to take a trip together. It's the perfect
ending to a day spent birdwatching at the Jamaica
Bay Wildlife Refuge (see page 46).

Although jackets are not required, people tend to
dress up here on Friday and Saturday nights, and
the restaurant is filled with young couples on
important dates or celebrating birthdays (this is
the kind of place where the waiters make a big

production over your birthday and gather 'round in a group to sing to you). The menu is Continental and specializes in pasta, veal, seafood, and steaks. The food varies from adequate to wonderful, but I found the lobster to be exquisite. Start off with a selection from the antipasto cart and torture yourselves over the scrumptious dessert cart, or save yourselves the trouble and simply order the spectacular tableside flambés: cherries jubilee or bananas foster.

This is romance in the old style—single people crowded under the green cone lights above the bar; the piano player sitting in the corner in front of a brick wall and behind a huge display of flowers, serenading you with old standards and torch songs; and the two of you snuggling by the candlelight in your own little world.

Spend an hour before or after dinner strolling around the Canarsie Pier. If you remember how run down the pier was years ago, you'll be pleasantly surprised by the expensive refurbishment. Some people arrive at Abbracciamento by boat, where they dock on the newly renovated pier. Bird-watching by day, billing and cooing by night—that's what romance is all about.

Alley's End

ADDRESS: 311 WEST 17TH STREET, NEW YORK, NY 10011 (BETWEEN EIGHTH AND NINTH AVENUES) ♥ PHONE: 212-627-8899 ♥ HOURS: SUNDAY THROUGH THURSDAY 6:00 P.M. TO 11:00 P.M.; FRIDAY AND SATURDAY 6:00 P.M. TO 1:00 A.M. ♥ PRICE: EXPENSIVE

The business card of this lovably eccentric, casual establishment directs you there with an exclamation point: "An American bistro hideaway . . . just west of Eighth Avenue and down the alley!" Don't think for one minute that they're kidding. Even knowing the address you'll have trouble finding this restaurant in the little alley between buildings 301 and 311. All I can say is, don't give up; it's worth finding.

You'll first pass through the funky bar in front with its copper mesh ceiling. A pleasant person will lead you to one of the booths with a copper leaf table, or, space permitting, you may choose to sit in a little alcove beside the glass-enclosed outdoor rock garden where you can watch the fish swim in the pond. Candles will flicker red, blue, and green light on your smiling faces.

The very reasonably priced eclectic American menu will tempt you with such delicious creations as "sugar cane skewered grilled shrimp" served with "oven roasted pineapple and wilted spinach" and "tuna steak dusted with black pepper, nori wrapped and served with sweet rice and watercress, cucumber and pickled ginger."

While the food melts in your mouth, your ears will be filled with slow, jazzy vocals — Billie Holiday perhaps, or some other lilting, romantic music. You will always think of Alley's End as the secret place you found together.

The *Jefferson Market Garden* on Ninth Street just west of Sixth Avenue is a bit of a walk from Alley's End, but we did pass through on the way to our early dinner, and it did make for quite a romantic date. What you'll find is a small garden filled with lush greenery, flowers, and a little lily pond. It's kept up by local volunteers and, weather permitting, it's open on Wednesday, Saturday, and Sunday afternoons from approximately 2:00 to 5:30 P.M. The Greenwich Village Society for Historical Preservation calls it "a verdant blooming oasis in the heart of Greenwich Village." Who are we to argue? It's a great place for a first kiss . . . or a second.

*A*ureole

ADDRESS: 34 EAST 61ST STREET, NEW YORK, NY 10021 (BETWEEN PARK AND MADISON AVENUES) ♥ PHONE: 212-319-1660 ♥ HOURS: MONDAY THROUGH FRIDAY NOON TO 2:30 P.M. AND 5:30 P.M. TO 11:00 P.M.; SATURDAY 5:00 P.M. TO 11:30 P.M.; CLOSED SUNDAY ♥ PRIX FIXE DINNER; LUNCH IS À LA CARTE ♥ PRICE: VERY EXPENSIVE

If you want to impress the person you love most in the world (or the person you want most to love you), make a dinner reservation at Aureole. This is by far the best restaurant to choose if you are looking for the most sensual dining experience you can imagine.

Aureole in Latin means "halo," and once inside you will feel blessed. You'll feel blessed first by the décor, with its bas-relief wall art of wildlife set against a colorful explosion of the largest flower arrangements I've ever seen—a purposeful and simple elegance that has most of the diners passing up the outdoor garden in preference to the inside one. And you'll feel twice-blessed by the cuisine. Each dish, even the garden salad, is so beautifully presented that you may at first hesitate to eat it. But take just one bite, and you won't hesitate again. This is a restaurant that appeals to the senses—taste, sound, and sight—so strongly that you won't even mind the close tables or the prix fixe. It probably doesn't matter what you order. We had the carmelized Clark Farm chicken with sweet corn risotto and the sautéed veal medallions with carmelized chestnuts. Be sure to save room for dessert. The sculptured, origami-like desserts belong in the Museum of Modern Art. The service is gracious and attentive.

The mezzanine looks out over the beautiful main dining area—a perfect setting for a romantic interlude. Again, there is an outdoor garden that is open during the spring and summer months, but even on the loveliest day, you will probably find that indoors is the romantic place to be.

At 34 East 61st Street, you are only a block and a half from *Fifth Avenue* and the best place in the world for window shopping. Saks Fifth Avenue, Tiffany's, Bergdorf Goodman, and many of the designer stores are there (the rest are on *Madison*). You are also a pleasant stroll away from New York's "museum district." *The Museum Mile*, along Fifth Avenue, starts at 82nd Street with the *Metropolitan Museum of Art* (212-535-7710) and includes *Goethe House* (82nd Street; 212-439-8700); the *Solomon R. Guggenheim Museum* (88th Street; 212-423-3500) *National Academy of Design* (89th Street; 212-369-4880); the *Cooper-Hewitt Museum* (91st Street; 212-849-8400); the Jewish Museum (92nd Street; 212-423-3200); and the International Center of Photography (94th Street; 212-860-1777).

*B*allroom Dancing In and Around Manhattan

You've seen Fred Astaire and Ginger Rogers twirl their way through magnificently choreographed dance numbers, and you've probably wished that you and your partner could trip the light fantastic like that. Well, you can, even if you have two left feet and your wardrobes don't include tuxedos or the flowing, romantic gowns and spike heels that Ginger used to wear.

When people think of dinner and dancing in New York, they usually think of the Rainbow Room, but few people can afford that. Rainbow Room, move over, because dinner and dancing is in full swing all over the city and you're invited to join in the fun. For instance, it would be hard to find a more romantic and exquisite date than a summer evening at Lincoln Center. The ultimate dancing destination is *Midsummer Night's Swing under the Stars at Lincoln Center's Fountain Plaza* (inexpensive), where you and your partner can dance to the romantic sounds of live musicians playing in front of the world-famous Lincoln Center fountain. You've seen this location as the romantic backdrop in the movie *Moonstruck*—it's where the glamorously made-up Cher meets Nicolas Cage for their first date at the opera— and you can picture what a striking image you'll make as your own loved one gets a look at you next to that fountain. Float across the open-air "ballroom" as the music bounces off the buildings around you, and the sounds of the fountain will transport you to the piazzas of Rome. You might want to toss a coin and make a wish . . . even if that wish is only that you two don't trip over some of the more experienced ballroom dancers gliding past you.

If you can dance, it's the ultimate. Even if you can't dance, it's a wonderful place to be the worst at something. Although some people dress in jeans, many men wear tuxes and women often wear short skirts and lots of glitter. Hold your partner close in this open-air ballroom; Fred and Ginger will be smiling down on you. Call the Lincoln Center Fountain Plaza at 212-875-5766 for scheduling information.

On less-than-balmy nights, year-round, there are many other places you can dance in Manhattan. On Sunday nights, the *New York Swing Dance Society* meets to do the Lindy hop at 17 Irving Plaza at 15th Street. The doors open at 7:00 P.M., when you can dance to taped music, and the band plays from 8:00 P.M. until midnight. On the first Sunday of each month, the dance lesson from 7:00 P.M. to 8:00 P.M. is free. For more information and scheduling, call 212-NY-NYSDS. If you enjoy salsa, try the *Copacabana* at 617 West 57th Street. Call 212-582-COPA for scheduling and prices.

Intimidated by being the only beginner out there on the dance floor? Have a partner who is uncoordinated but willing to try? Then get yourselves to one of the many great dance studios in New York City. One is *Stepping Out* at 1780 Broadway at 57th Street, 212-245-5200. Another is the *Sandra Cameron Dance Center* at 20 Cooper Square, 212-674-0505, which hosts a special guest night on one Friday each month during which a free lesson and a party are held. In fact, many of the dance studios offer beginners' classes, with some being a short-term series of lessons and others lasting for six to eight weeks. Private lessons are mixed with Friday-night social dances, and partners are encouraged to come to these parties dressed in their finest. If you're a new dancer, you might find yourself a little intimidated by some of the more-experienced couples. Just remember, they're not looking at you. Like you, they're looking at the best dancers on the floor, the ones who are really shaking it and making it fly out there. So when you and your partner trip over each other, just laugh and keep smiling. As long as you don't take it too seriously, you'll be having more fun than anybody else.

Once you have your basic moves down, it may be time to celebrate at the granddaddy of all romantic dancing locales—the aforementioned Rainbow Room. Located at 30 Rockefeller Plaza at Rockefeller Center (212-632-5000), the Rainbow Room is the ultimate in destinations. Everyone ought to visit here at least once in a lifetime. The prices are steep, but the memories will be worth it. This dark, romantic venue is set high atop the city, with windows all around so that the sky-scrapers and the nighttime stars are the backdrop to your own mini–production number. The lighting is dim, and there are points of light at each table, where you may choose to sit with your sweetheart until the dancing portion of the evening starts. Often, you'll be dancing to the sounds of live entertainers, and you may be treated to a show by some of Broadway's best talent. Hit the dance floor and sway to the music of the city's next big shooting star, and see the stars twinkle just for the two of you as you move together at the top of the city, the heart of the city's nightlife. The rest of the crowd will melt away, and it will be just you and your partner in each other's arms, moving as one. Dress is formal here and jackets are required, so dress to the nines and join the beautiful people for a spin at one of the most exclusive spots in town.

In the winter months, you might choose to begin your romantic evening at the Rainbow Room by watching the ice skaters at Rockefeller Center. There is almost always someone out there who moves as gracefully as an Olympic figure skater, and he or she might put you in the mood to do some fancy footwork of your own upstairs. End your big night by walking through the underground shopping center beneath Rockefeller Center and finding a memento of your visit to the Rainbow Room.

In the winter months, take your dancing lessons to the ice. Try your balance and skill at the Rockefeller Center skating rink (inexpensive), or don some skates and glide across the frozen surface of Wollman Rink in Central Park (inexpensive). For Wollman Rink's ice skating hours, prices, and information, call 212-396-1010. Feel the cold wind on your face as you hold hands and skate wide circles together, marveling at the fancy moves you see all around you. Not only is this type of evening fun and romantic, it's also a lot of exercise, a great way for you and your partner to stay in shape together. Plus, it's fun to topple over in a heap, steal a quick kiss, and get up and start all over again.

Still one more night of dining and dancing can be found on a *World Yacht Cruise* (212-630-8100), which sets sail each night from West 41st Street and the Hudson River. Dining, dancing, a three-hour cruise around the southern tip of Manhattan, watching the sun set behind the Statue of Liberty . . . how much better does life get?

*B*ed and Breakfast on the Park

ADDRESS: 113 PROSPECT PARK WEST, PARK SLOPE, BROOKLYN, NY 11215 ♥ PHONE: 718-499-6115 ♥ FOOD: A SPECTACULARLY BIG BREAKFAST ♥ PRICE: MODERATE

Given the opportunity to travel back in time, which period of history and what place would you most like to journey to? For me, there is no contest: turn-of-the-century New York.

What if I told you you could travel to just such a time and place? Well, almost. Bed and Breakfast on the Park is the closest thing you're likely to find to a time machine.

"More Victorian than London! More lovely than home!" said one London couple after a stay at Bed and Breakfast on the Park.

Our favorite room? (Yes, we peeked at all of them!) The Grande Victoria. Two bedrooms, private bath, cable TV (which, of course, you'll keep tuned to the "romance" channel, if you dare turn it on). But the bald facts cannot begin to describe the charm (it is amazing how this inn made us both long for a time we had never experienced). We were waxing nostalgic while sitting under the stained-glass windows, amid the intricately carved oak molding, and the Victorian antiques, beside the wood-burning fireplace, wondering whether the art of kissing had changed much in a hundred years.

The Grande Victoria may be a bit outside your price range, but don't despair. The Garden Suite is just as charming, only smaller, and more affordable.

Bed and Breakfast on the Park faces *Prospect Park*, where one can go boating on the lake in warm weather or just stroll around and enjoy the pastoral beauty. It's also only a 20-minute walk from the Brooklyn Museum of Art and the *Brooklyn Botanic Garden* (see Brooklyn Botanic Garden listing). When leaving the bed and breakfast, simply turn left and walk north along the park to the far north corner. You'll be able to see the Museum ahead and to the right.

And you won't want to miss gazing at each other across a casual meal at *Dizzy's* around the corner at 511 Ninth Street (718-499-1966), where the fifties diner décor, Frank Sinatra music, and day and night comfort food will relax you into quiet contemplation of each other.

$\mathcal{T}$he Box Tree

ADDRESS: 250 EAST 49TH STREET, NEW YORK, NY 10017
(BETWEEN SECOND AND THIRD AVENUES) ♥ PHONE: 212-758-8320 ♥
HOURS: MONDAY THROUGH FRIDAY 12:30 P.M. TO 3:00 P.M. AND
5:30 P.M. TO 10:00 P.M.; SATURDAY AND SUNDAY 5:30 P.M. TO 10:00 P.M.
♥ DRESS: JACKETS REQUIRED; TIES OPTIONAL; NO SNEAKERS OR JEANS.
♥ RESERVATIONS REQUIRED ♥ PRICE: EXPENSIVE

The Box Tree is a quaint, romantic combination restaurant–bed and breakfast with different flavors for every mood. You'll enter a different world as you step into the English foyer, and you'll feel as if you've entered an accommodating castle when you reach the enormous carved fireplace of the St. Jerome Room. The bar area boasts turn-of-the-century woodwork and impressive Dutch architecture. The main dining room has an English flair, complete with artwork and décor that will make you think you're in the manse of your dreams.

If money is no object, perhaps you'll want to secure one of the three private dining rooms upstairs, each with its own romantic style. The Music Room has a beautiful, roaring fireplace and elegant Tiffany windows through which you can view the sunset. The Blue Room also offers a fireplace and is filled with eye-catching and conversation-starting art nouveau. The Gold Room is a palace unto itself, with its French and Versailles-like touches. For a trip to Europe, without the air fare, join your hosts at the Box Tree for a romantic escape back in time.

As impressive as the décor is, it pales in comparison with the chef's menu, which varies according to season. Included in the appetizers are snails in Pernod butter gratinée, house-cured salmon, terrine of duck liver with foie gras, and blini with salmon caviar and chilled vodka. Follow that course with a Maine lobster bisque or any of the other delectable soups, and go on to sample the pecan-crusted red snapper, the rack of lamb with fresh mint sauce, or the roasted pheasant with juniper berries. Finish off the meal with chocolate praline wafers, assorted fresh berries, delice au chocolat, or crème brûlée.

The Box Tree's prix fixe dinner includes three or five courses. For lunch, you can choose between a three-course or an à la carte menu.

The Box Tree's menu and décor take you to another time and place, which is what makes it such a romantic escape from the everyday sights and sounds of the city. After your meal, you may want to walk off those calories with a stroll east to the park by the river at *Sutton Terrace*, which would give you another excuse to hold hands and enjoy the scenic views as you go along.

$\mathcal{B}$ridgeton House

ADDRESS: 1525 River Road (Route 32), Upper Black Eddy, Pennsylvania 18972 ♥ **PHONE:** 610-982-5856 ♥ All rooms have air conditioning and private baths (some with tubs). ♥ **DIRECTIONS:** Take the Holland Tunnel to the New Jersey Turnpike South to exit 14 (Newark Airport). Follow the signs for Route 78 West. Take 78 West to exit 15 (Clinton/Pittstown). Exit and turn left at the light onto Route 513 South. Follow Route 513 South into Frenchtown. Cross the bridge into Pennsylvania. Turn right, and it's three miles upriver (north) on the righthand side. The trip should take about one hour and 15 minutes. ♥ **PRICE:** Moderate

Need to unwind for a few days? I know just the place. It's called the Bridgeton House because it overlooks a bridge over the Delaware River to New Jersey, right across from the charming little town of Milford, and many guests proclaim it to be the nicest place they've ever stayed. It's guaranteed to take the city out of you in an instant, and isn't it about time you had a good night's sleep?

Bridgeton House is a lovable inn decorated whimsically and brightly with pastels and deep reds; every room of the old house is filled with comfortable and eye-pleasing antiques. The beds are comfortable and just small enough to make cuddling necessary. The three-course gourmet breakfast will fill you up for the day. There are so many original foods to choose from on the menu (which itself is unusual at a B&B) that you're just going to have to share in order to taste everything.

Rooms face either River Road or the river. The river rooms have French doors that open onto private, screened-in porches. In the summer, you can sit on rocking chairs on your porch or the inn's porch and watch the boats, tubes, rafts, kayaks, and canoes floating by. Or better yet, join them. Contact *River Country* for information about summer river activities (P.O. Box 6, Point Pleasant, PA 18950; 215-297-5000). They'll also tell you about fall hayrides and can provide outdoor wedding information, too.

Because, as lovely as it is, the best thing about the Bridgeton House is its location and the plethora of nearby activities—and not just on the river. First, take a long, mind-clearing walk along the tow path that runs alongside the *Delaware Canal* (a 60-mile state park) for many, many miles. Stop for some refreshment and to pet the Dalmatians at the *General Store*. Later in the day, drive to nearby Frenchtown and rent bicycles from *Freeman's Bicycle Shop* (52 Bridge Street, Frenchtown, NJ 08825; 908-996-7712). Ride on the cinder path along the *Delaware River*; it's flat and straight. Weather permitting, you may want to take a dip. When you return to *Frenchtown*, treat yourselves to some cones, sodas, or cappuccinos at *Buck's Ice Cream & Espresso Bar* (52 Bridge Street, Frenchtown, NJ 08825; 908-996-7258).

Take a scenic drive north along the Delaware to the *Delaware Water Gap* or South to the charming towns of *New Hope*, Pennsylvania, and (across the river) *Lambertville*, New Jersey, where you can get lost in the many antique, gift, and craft shops. Frenchtown, too, has a lot of fun places to shop.

The Bridgeton House keeps a selection of menus of nearby restaurants, and the owners are happy to make recommendations, depending on your particular cravings and budget. *Chef Tell's Manor House* on the Delaware (1800 River Road, Upper Black Eddy, PA 18972; 1-800-4CHEF-TL) is expensive but has excellent Continental food, such as filet mignon and baked shrimp, and also some German specialties, such as Wiener schnitzel with spaetzle and sauerbraten.

Brooklyn Botanic Garden

ADDRESS: 1000 WASHINGTON AVENUE, BROOKLYN, NY 11225 ♥
WEB ADDRESS: WWW.BBG.ORG ♥ **PHONE:** 718-623-7200 ♥
PRICE: INEXPENSIVE

The Brooklyn Botanic Garden is an oasis in the midst of Flatbush and a perfect place for a Saturday or Sunday outing. Dine in the Terrace Café near the Steinhardt Conservatory and take a romantic stroll through the Cherry Esplanade, a long rectangle of open and shaded lawn where visitors are allowed to walk and laze about.

Rather than enter the garden at the parking lot gate at Washington Avenue or the main entrance at Eastern Parkway, enter at the Flatbush Avenue gate, the corner of Flatbush and Empire Boulevards. You will be seeing the garden in reverse of how most visitors see it, but the garden is immense and sprawling—there is no one single route to follow, as you will see once you are there. You will want to go backward through the Garden for two reasons. One, the Cherry Esplanade will be towards the end, where you most likely will want to stop and rest. Two, if you exit the garden through the Eastern Parkway Gate, you will come out beside the Brooklyn Museum of Art (200 Eastern Parkway at Washington Avenue, Brooklyn, NY 11213; 718-638-5000), the second leg of your outing.

Highlights of the garden: near where you will be entering, the Children's Garden (yes, planted and tended by children); the Conservatory, which contains all manner of exotic flora in controlled environments; the Japanese Hill-and-Pond Garden; the Cranford Rose Garden, which contains so many hybrids that the names for them are amusing in and of themselves; and the Rock Garden. Just past the Rock Garden, to your right on the way to the entrance gate, is the most enchanting weeping willow tree. Stepping through its curtain of hanging fronds, you are likely to recall some secret hiding place of your youth. As the seasons change, so does the garden. Walk arm in arm along the Cherry Esplanade during cherry blossom season or choose a less popular time of year to go together. Rest and kiss under the trees along the Cherry Esplanade, then continue on to the Eastern Parkway gate. To your right is the entrance to the Brooklyn Museum of Art. The museum has an excellent collection of Rodin sculptures, as well as Native American exhibits—and that is just a tiny part of what it has to offer.

Brooklyn Bridge and the Promenade

There are two ways to take advantage of the *Brooklyn Bridge*: a day walk or an evening walk. The most impressive view is toward Manhattan, so take the subway to Brooklyn. The A, 2, 3, 4, or R trains will drop you in the vicinity of Cadman and Walt Whitman Parks, which border *Brooklyn Heights*.

During the day, walk together through Cadman Park toward Brooklyn Heights, and wander along any of the quaint streets—Poplar, Cranberry, or Clark—toward Upper New York Bay and the Promenade. Stroll arm in arm along the brick walkway, past little yards and gardens on one side of the Promenade and the East River on the other. Sit and take in the view of downtown Manhattan and the Statue of Liberty in the distance. Along *Henry Street* you can stop off at *Sipp's* for tea or ice cream (try to get that cushy leather sofa at the window). For something more substantial, *Noodle Pudding* (718-625-3737), also on Henry Street, is a good bet. Then enter the Brooklyn Bridge at the northeast corner of Cadman Park. Late afternoon or evening is the best time for this walk back to the city. You can rest along the way on one of the benches and watch the sky turn various shades of orange to the south as the sun sets behind the downtown skyline and admire the city lights. (Note: Be sure to keep to the north side of the yellow line as you walk along the bridge. The south side is the biking lane.)

For an evening excursion, plan dinner at the *River Café* at 1 Water Street (718-522-5200), directly under the bridge, or, for a fraction of the cost, at *Pete's* at One Old Fulton Street (718-858-3510). Both restaurants have wonderful food (Pete's has Italian), but the River Café has the deck and one of the most spectacular sunset dining views in the city. If you don't sit outside, request a seat by the window. (Be advised: The River Café is expensive, and jackets are required for dinner. No jeans or sneakers, but remember you'll want comfortable shoes for the stroll over the bridge.) To get there, walk along Washington Street to the north side of the bridge. Old Fulton will bring you to the river. The River Café has a little wooden deck out front with benches and flowers; a nice place to relax after dinner and before heading for the bridge.

If you have time, try to include a stroll through the *Fulton Ferry State Park*. This little out-of-the-way park can be found by passing through the black iron gates north of the River Café entrance and walking around the base of the Brooklyn Bridge. (Incidentally, it's from this spot under the bridge that you will get the most impressive view of the bridge, the river, and the Manhattan skyline.) The Fulton Ferry State Park has some most unusual sculptures and a boardwalk right on the bank. Also, this may be the only place in New York where you can listen to the water beating against the rocks. The East River empties into the Bay here, and the water is alive with sailboats, yachts, tourist ferries, and jet skis. But the park closes at 8:00 P.M., so take advantage of it before dinner if you can.

After dinner, enter the Brooklyn Bridge from Washington Street. There is something about approaching Manhattan at a leisurely pace along a board-walk that makes the entire city seem "graspable"—a romantic notion if ever there was one.

$\mathcal{B}$ryant Park

RIGHT BEHIND THE NEW YORK PUBLIC LIBRARY AND BORDERED BY 40TH STREET, 42ND STREET, FIFTH, AND SIXTH AVENUES ♥ PRICE: INEXPENSIVE

If you're looking for a place to stroll quietly or picnic in the center of midtown Manhattan, you could not do better than Bryant Park. If you haven't been to Bryant Park since it enjoyed a reputation as a place rife with drugs and crime, you're in for a great surprise. Miraculously trans-formed into a Parisian-style park, it will make you feel, as you walk down its wide pathways, very much as though you're making your way from the Champs-Elysées to the Tuileries. Season and weather permitting, expect to see lots of flowers, ivy covered trees, chairs scattered here and there for you to sit in, chess players, people reading, busi-nesspeople eating their lunches, and groups of all ages talking in small clusters. Picnic on the big, grassy lawn or sit on or near the imposing multilevel granite fountain and pool or in another spot that suits the two of you. On summer nights, spread a blanket and watch an old classic movie on a gigantic screen. You can bring your picnic or buy some delicious and inexpensive sandwiches, fresh pasta, soups, and ice cream from one of the two kiosks that flank the fountain.

At these prices, you don't have to live on love. One of the kiosks is open May through October from 8:00 A.M. to dusk and the other is open year-round during the same hours. The one that's open year-round has excellent coffee, espresso, and latté and an iced mocha that the *New York Times* has called "the sexiest drink in New York." Just a block north—and a stone's throw east—is *Flowers Naturally* (37 West 43rd Street; 212-302-4090), a wonderful little florist. Go in and breathe deeply; then buy a rose for your sweetheart. On the outskirts of the park are signs listing summer events such as summer afternoon jazz and classical concerts, Wednesday night dance and theater performances and Monday night movies in the park.

If the weather isn't good or you're looking for a real restaurant, try the *Bryant Park Grill*, 25 West 40th Street, New York 10018 (212-840-6500). It's a very nice, spacious restaurant, but not so romantic that you would choose it to propose. The food is among New York's best, and it's a very comfortable restaurant to dine in, the kind you'll want to go back to often. It's open for lunch and dinner seven days, and there are several outdoor seating areas: a roof garden, a casual café (inexpensive) with a lighter, less expensive menu, and an outdoor grill (expensive). The roof garden and outdoor café menus include sandwiches such as "old-fashioned chicken salad" and entreés such as vegetarian pasta salad. The Bryant Park Grill itself is more expensive and entreés include chilled lobster, chopped vegetable salad, and herb-crusted filet mignon. Dinner entreés include such pleasures as soft-shell crabs and hazelnut-crusted rack of lamb. On the weekend, your fixed price brunch might include fresh asparagus frittata with roasted Yukon Gold potatoes and fontina cheese, or brioche French toast. Call ahead because there are lots of private parties on the weekend.

Whether you eat indoors or outdoors, picnic, or just stroll, take a peek inside the magnificent *New York Public Library* (Fifth Avenue and 42nd Street)—as much a museum as a library. Enjoy the current exhibits, find a corner to smooch in, read some racy manuscripts or poetry together, and whisper sweet nothings into each others' ears. The recently renovated Rose Main Reading Room on the third floor is an awesome sight, not to be missed. The cupids on the ceiling are especially romantic. Don't walk and kiss at the same time.

*C*afé des Artistes

ADDRESS: ONE WEST 67TH STREET, NEW YORK, NY 10023 (BETWEEN CENTRAL PARK WEST AND COLUMBUS AVENUE) ♥ **PHONE:** 212-877-3500 ♥ **HOURS:** MONDAY THROUGH FRIDAY NOON TO 2:45 P.M. AND 5:30 P.M. TO 11:45 P.M.; SATURDAY AND SUNDAY 10:00 A.M. TO 2:45 P.M. (BRUNCH) AND 5:30 P.M. TO 11:45 P.M. ♥ **DRESS:** JACKETS REQUIRED; NO JEANS OR SNEAKERS ♥ **RESERVATIONS** RECOMMENDED—SEVERAL DAYS IN ADVANCE, OR A FEW WEEKS AHEAD FOR FRIDAY OR SATURDAY EVENING ♥ **PRICE:** EXPENSIVE

This is Manhattan-style romance—costly, perhaps, but a French restaurant experience that should not be missed. Café des Artistes is not exactly a New York secret, but neither is it overrun with tourists, in spite of the fact that on any given evening you are likely to find yourselves dining a couple of tables away from one well-known personality or another. If celebrity-spotting of the opera and theater crowd appeals to you, Café des Artistes will provide those thrills as you peek at the performers over your menus.

To get to Café des Artistes, we would suggest grabbing a taxi from wherever you are, but if you prefer the subway, and if you have left yourselves time, get off at Columbus Circle and stroll up the park side of Central Park West until you arrive at the restaurant. Then, step into an elegant décor of sumptuous flowers and richly muted murals of bathing nymphs—all of which look curiously alike. For an expensive French restaurant in New York, the service is surprisingly attentive. The waiters are knowledgeable and are quick to recommend or describe a dish. The desserts are exquisite.

After dinner, if the weather is nice and it isn't too late in the evening, take a stroll into *Central Park* at the 72nd Street entrance. Walk to the open amphitheater; sit in front of the fountain, and watch the inline skaters. You can get to the southernmost end of the park, at 59th Street, by walking down the tree-lined esplanade. Then stroll along *Central Park South*, stopping wherever the spirit moves you. Or maybe stop for spirits at *Fantino* (112 Central Park South, New York, NY 10019, between Sixth and Seventh Avenues; 212-664-7700), which used to be the Jockey Bar at the former Ritz-Carlton Hotel.

Café Pierre and Rotunda at the Pierre Hotel

ADDRESS: TWO EAST 61ST STREET, NEW YORK, NY 10021 (BETWEEN FIFTH AND MADISON AVENUES) ♥ PHONE: 212-838-8000 ♥ HOURS: BREAKFAST, LUNCH, AND DINNER SEVEN DAYS; SUNDAY BRUNCH NOON TO 2:30 P.M. EITHER IN CAFÉ PIERRE OR ROTUNDA; AFTERNOON TEA SEVEN DAYS IN ROTUNDA 3:00 P.M. TO 5:30 P.M.; COCKTAILS IN ROTUNDA AND IN THE BAR 6:30 P.M. TO MIDNIGHT. ♥ RESERVATIONS STRONGLY RECOMMENDED FOR THE CAFÉ; NO RESERVATIONS TAKEN FOR THE ROTUNDA FOR ANY MEAL, INCLUDING AFTERNOON TEA

The Café Pierre (expensive) is not a café at all but rather is a fine and intimate restaurant. Enter it through the *Rotunda* (very expensive) or the Pierre Lounge. In the foyer, at the intersection of the three unique rooms, the maitre d' stands ready to greet you before circular trompe l'oeil murals that appear to be windows looking out onto Magritte skies. Near him, a pianist, who arrives every night at 8:30, effortlessly taps out light jazz, Cole Porter, and quiet ballads, sometimes singing in a lilting, sexy voice. Fragrant white lilies spill out over their branches. If you haven't come to propose, be careful; by the end of the evening, you'll probably want to.

The small, softly lit room, with fewer than 20 tables, has a European feel. There are many comfortable banquettes to choose from, and every table is the best. Each one is set with a random variety of fabulous china plates in different patterns, silver salt and pepper shakers, and a small bouquet of flowers. Gold-leaf lampshades top real candles.

You'll look around the eggshell-colored room at the lace curtains, gold draperies, ornate mirrors, and elegantly dressed people, and you'll think perhaps you're dining in the king's chambers. In fact, you'll know it, once the food starts arriving. Although some light entreés are offered, this is not an evening to be on a diet.

The wine list is varied and impressive, as you would expect, and the menu is imaginative and seductive. The chef will present you with a treat to start with, perhaps a little swordfish tart. Then comes the selection of breads and Parmesan toast. The fois gras will melt in your mouth; the lobster fricassee will put you in heaven. The desserts are worth every golden bite, and you may choose to have them served to you in the adjoining Rotunda, or retire there afterwards for a glass of fine port or, if you're into it, a cigar.

If this is all too much for you, or too early, lighter food is offered every night on the supper menu from 10:00 to 11:00 P.M. From the supper menu choose such entreés as tagliatelle with lobster, morels, asparagus, and citrus sauce, or Charles Pierre scrambled eggs with smoked salmon and caviar.

Spending time in the opulent *Rotunda* (very expensive) before or after dinner—or instead, for a meal, cocktails, dessert, brunch, or afternoon tea—is an experience that should not be missed. A circular extravaganza of a room featuring a two-sided granite staircase, its walls and ceilings ornately decorated with colorful but muted trompe l'oeil murals. The room is lit softly at night with wall candelabras and more brightly during the day. In the center of it all is the largest profusion of flowers you may ever have seen. Sit together on one of the tiny loveseats that surround the room, sip champagne, listen to the classical music, point out things in the murals, and tell each other how much you've come to mean to each other.

English afternoon tea at the Rotunda includes assorted tea sandwiches, freshly baked scones with Devonshire cream, preserves, a selection of tea savories, and your choice of over 20 teas and Starbucks gourmet coffees.

The Carlyle Hotel

ADDRESS: 35 EAST 76TH STREET, NEW YORK, NY 10021 (BETWEEN MADISON AND PARK AVENUES) ♥ **PHONE:** 212-744-1600 ♥ **PRICE:** VERY EXPENSIVE

For sheer old New York black-and-white movie glamour, almost nothing beats the Carlyle Hotel and all of its swank nightspots. From October to New Year's Eve, the Café Carlyle is home to singer-pianist Bobby Short, whose throaty renditions of Cole Porter have been entertaining the elegant set there since 1967. When Bobby Short is not around, entertainers such as Eartha Kitt, Dixie Carter, and Barbara Cook hold sway. It's not a cheap night out, but it's worthwhile and memorable. Short charms the crowd (which tends to be slightly older). There is almost always fun celebrity-spotting, and for a little while you are transported to the New York of Nick and Nora Charles—and aren't they the ultimate romantic couple?

For a nightcap, move on to the Carlyle's Bemelmans Bar, and, yes, the same Ludwig Bemelmans who wrote and illustrated the enchanting Madeline series of children's books painted the equally enchanting murals of his namesake bar. Bemelmans, who was in the hotel and restaurant business before he became a writer, wrote mildly satirical sketches with illustrations of a posh hotel much like the Carlyle called the Hotel Splendide for the *New Yorker* in the 1930s and 1940s. And, no, you haven't had too many drinks; those *are* well-dressed rabbits imbibing cocktails along with humans and other animals ice-skating along the walls of this whimsical boîte. From 9:45 P.M. to 12:45 A.M., there is music by Peter Mintun or Barbara Carroll. There's music Tuesday through Saturday (call for schedule).

The ultimate end to your date, of course, would be a night in a room at the Carlyle (where JFK allegedly used to tryst with Marilyn). Again, this is a splurge, but the Carlyle is one of my favorite romantic hotels in New York. It's elegant, tasteful, solicitous but never haughty. The rooms are all beautifully appointed in English style, some by well-known decorator Mark Hampton. For an anniversary or an extremely special night on the town, it's worth every precious penny. Of course, if you don't have that many pennies, opt for afternoon tea at the Carlyle's Gallery, served seven days a week from 3:00 to 5:30 P.M. This traditional afternoon tea served at cozy little tables will give you the full flavor of the Carlyle without as much pressure on your purse.

Caumsett State Park, Lloyd Neck, Long Island

DIRECTIONS: TAKE THE LONG ISLAND EXPRESSWAY TO ROUTE 110 NORTH TO HUNTINGTON. THIS BECOMES NEW YORK AVENUE ONCE YOU'RE IN HUNTINGTON. MAKE A LEFT ON MAIN STREET (25A). YOU WILL GO THROUGH THE TOWN, PASSING BY MANY FINE SHOPS. MAKE A RIGHT ON WEST NECK ROAD AND GO FIVE MILES TO THE PARK.

If you're looking for a potentially secluded spot far from the noises of civilization, Caumsett State Park may very well be the place for you.

It's a good idea either to eat before you get to the park or to plan on a picnic, since no real food is provided (a few machines are available). There are no designated areas set up specifically for picnicking, but there is a plethora of grassy areas just begging for a blanket. If you pick your spot right, you'll be disturbed only by the plaintive cries of Canadian geese in the summer. A three-mile walking trail awaits.

It's a lovely, peaceful walk, on smooth ground, first through an open area and then in and out of forestlike settings. On the particular summer weekday afternoon we chose, we were at times alone, content with the feeling of remoteness and tranquillity that comes from a walk in the country.

In the autumn, around the last week of October, it is an absolutely exquisite setting. One wonderful peaking fall day showcased an astounding number of brilliant red leaves mixing with the customary oranges and yellows. (Of course, each year's foliage display depends on the weather conditions during the preceding spring and summer.) As you continue on the path, you'll come to another open field, suitable for Frisbee and other assorted frolicking. Many people do choose to bike-ride along this path; inline skating is not allowed.

About a mile and half from the beginning, you will come to an extraordinarily picturesque view of Long Island Sound, replete with sailboats off in the distance. On autumn weekends, the grassy field overlooking the water may be less than solitary, with many partaking of the view. Weekday getaways hold the potential for more secluded and romantic viewing. From that spot, walk down the hillside (the left route is easier), and if you go left at the fresh water pond, you'll encounter a bridle path. Loop around and before you know it, you will be right on the beach. It's a rocky beach—an enchanting beach, but not really one for swimming. Collect the unique shells and rocks that seem to come from faraway shores. You can also have fun climbing on the rocks that jut out into the Sound. You can either retrace your steps or continue the loop around. Another mile and a half gets you to the parking lot.

Caumsett State Park is a place for all seasons, including the winter. It happens to be very popular for cross country skiing, since it has so many open fields and gentle slopes. Whatever the season, Caumsett offers a romantic remoteness and serenity far from city sounds and sights.

Central Park

I could write a book about the 52 most romantic places in and around Central Park and still have enough entries left over for a second edition. Central Park is a spectacular work of art that keeps getting more spectacular. I will tell you some of my favorite spots that just call out to be shared. The *Central Park Wildlife Center* (near Fifth Avenue and East 64th Street) is a must-see for animal lovers. Watch the monkeys jumping around, see the seals getting fed, walk through a tropical rain forest and spot birds together. If you haven't been to the northern end of the park or if you haven't been there in a while, you must see the *Conservatory Garden* at Fifth Avenue and 105th Street, and don't miss the *Harlem Meer* in the northeast corner of the park. A particularly good way to see a lot of the park in one day is by bicycle. They're available to rent just north of the *Boathouse Café* (near East 76th Street). To my eyes, at least by daylight, all 840 acres are paradise. Hike in the northern woods. Hold hands on the balcony above the Wollman Rink. Go inline skating around the *Park Drive*. Rent a boat from the *Loeb Boathouse* (near 72nd Street). Watch the dogs frolic in the *Bethesda Fountain* (mid-park at 72nd Street). Stroll to the *Belvedere Castle* (mid-park at 79th) and climb up the winding staircases to the top. Pretend you're the king and queen of the surrounding land. Find the Turtle Pond, Strawberry Fields, the Shakespeare

Garden, and the Swedish Cottage. Be sure to see as many stunning monuments, statues, bridges, and gardens as you can. How ever often you visit the park, be assured you will not see the same park twice. On almost any day of the year, Central Park is the place to kindle or rekindle love.

If you're a cuddly couple, start the day off at F.A.O. Schwarz (767 Fifth Avenue, New York, NY 10022; 212-644-9400), where many of the stuffed animals are about your size and each toy-filled floor will make you more and more nostalgic. Find the toys you each played with as children—but this time, you'll want to share.

*C*hart House

ADDRESS: PIER D/T LINCOLN HARBOR, WEEHAWKEN, NJ 07087 ♥
PHONE: 201-348-6628 ♥ HOURS: MONDAY THROUGH THURSDAY
5:00 P.M. TO 10:00 P.M.; FRIDAY 5:00 P.M. TO 11:00 P.M.; SATURDAY
4:00 P.M. TO 11:00 P.M.; SUNDAY 4:00 P.M. TO 10:00 P.M. ♥
PRICE: EXPENSIVE

There's nothing like a view to enhance a delicious dining experience. With floor to ceiling glass panels on two levels of this very large restaurant on the water, the Chart House simply owns the New York skyline, and every seat within commands a view of it. Although it's a spacious restaurant, it feels intimate and not massive. You may not reserve a window seat, but do request one. The Chart House has a mouth-watering Continental menu, serving fabulous preparations such as sesame crusted salmon, all kinds of steaks, and several cuts of prime rib. It's one of the few chain restaurants that are consistently excellent. The sunset is not visible from the restaurant, because the windows face east, but the view is always remarkable, and when the sun goes down and the lights start to twinkle on the buildings, you'll know why people love New York. After dinner, it's fun to walk around the restaurant and see the views from all the windows. The bar area has a few comfortable couches. In fact, it's a nice place to just go and have a drink when you're not hungry.

Arrive by car if you can, because then it will be easy for you to drive up the hill to *Hamilton Park* in *Weehawken*, which is the southernmost park in a series that extends the length of *Boulevard East*. Because it's higher than the Chart House, unobstructed, and outdoors, the park provides an even more sweeping view of New York City. Cuddle up and gaze out together, or take a leisurely stroll, exercising both your feet and your lips. If you're not interested in dining at the Chart House, go to Hamilton Park anyway, any time of the year.

If you don't have a car, all is not lost. Take the *NY Waterway Ferry* (inexpensive; 1-800-53-FERRY) from Pier 78 on the Hudson River at West 38th Street to Port Imperial and taxi over to either the Chart House or Hamilton Park (try Rose Taxi Cab, 201-662-8524). There's a fine restaurant at Port Imperial called *Arthur's Landing* (Pershing Circle, Weehawken, NJ 07087; 201-867-0777, or from New York call 1-800-835-6060), but for the view and the food, I prefer the Chart House. Sometimes you can take a ferry directly to Lincoln Harbor and walk over to the Chart House; it will depend on the ferry timetable.

The ferry itself is a pleasant excursion, not to be missed. You'll notice that NY Waterway offers a variety of marvelous cruises. The 90-minute *New York Harbor Cruise* will give you an overview of the New York skyline, including the Chrysler Building and the Empire State Building, and you'll pass right by the Statue of Liberty. Or consider taking the *Twilight Cruise*, which features the bright lights of New York at night. The *Kykuit Cruise* to the Rockefeller Estate is a full seven-hour day and includes a tour of historic *Philipsburg Manor*, which is a working seventeenth-century Dutch Colonial farm and grist mill. The *Sleepy Hollow Cruise* is another seven-hour day, past the Palisades to Tarrytown. It, too, includes a visit to Philipsburg Manor, but it also features a trip to *Sunnyside*, the riverside home of Washington Irving. These cruises all depart from Pier 78 at West 38th Street on the Hudson.

*C*hez Le Chef (Frédéric) and Breakfast in Bed

ADDRESS: 127 LEXINGTON AVENUE, NEW YORK, NY 10016 (BETWEEN 28TH AND 29TH STREETS) ♥ PHONE: 212-685-1888 ♥ HOURS: WEEKDAYS 7:00 A.M. TO 11:00 P.M.; WEEKENDS 8:00 A.M. TO 11:00 P.M. ♥ PRICE: EXPENSIVE

Here's a great little casual café date—the perfect place for breakfast, brunch, or a late supper, and a fine choice for a casual dinner, too. But it's simply required that you're into food and that you go there hungry, because nothing gives the charming and eccentric Chef Frédéric more pleasure than to feed you.

Chez Le Chef is a bistro upstairs and a patisserie downstairs. The patisserie presents a feast for the eyes consisting of revolving desserts: muffins; Danish; pain aux raisins; brioche; pain perdu (don't miss trying this original French toast invention, hot and crunchy on the outside and soft inside!); carmelized palmiers; extravagant custom cakes (ask the chef to show you his book of cakes). Nowhere in town is there a better or more impressive bakery, and in the back you can look through the glass together and watch Frédéric, in his tall chef's hat and huge white handlebar moustache, turn out colorful confection after confection or put the finishing berries on his latest gooey masterpiece.

Serving more than just desserts, the whimsically decorated bistro upstairs has a huge, ever-changing menu of homemade wonders that include crepes, sandwiches, fresh soups and salads, homemade breads, and fondues (Did you know that if you drop your square of food in the fondu, it is traditional to kiss? —but you don't need an excuse, I know). Order your food downstairs and they'll bring it upstairs to you. Chez Le Chef is open all day for breakfast, lunch, dinner, dessert, or a snack, and Chef Frédéric will even cook you things that are not on the menu. You'll be dreaming about hot cider, potato pancakes, homemade jam, bananas and mangos in chocolate fondu, skinless chicken and fish fondues, souflees, canapes, pâtés —are you getting hungry yet?

All that said, here's the really special event: *Breakfast in Bed*. Order a basket filled with the Chef's creations and he'll package it all beautifully with a fresh rose and have it delivered to your door. Your basket might include some croissants, Danish, cappuccinos, fresh orange juice, a small bottle of champagne, cheese, pâtés, heart-shaped cookies, and pain perdu. The cost includes the basket, packaging, ribbons, and the card plus the exact cost of what you fill it up with and one way taxi fare anywhere in Manhattan (free delivery within five blocks). What's better than breakfast in bed? Don't answer that.

The Cloisters, Fort Tryon Park

ADDRESS: FORT TRYON PARK AT 192ND STREET, NEW YORK, NY 10040 (BETWEEN RIVERSIDE DRIVE AND FORT WASHINGTON AVENUE) ♥ **PHONE:** 212-923-3700 ♥ **HOURS:** TUESDAY THROUGH SUNDAY 9:30 A.M. TO 5:15 P.M. (MARCH–OCTOBER); 9:30 A.M. TO 4:45 P.M. (NOVEMBER–FEBRUARY) ♥ **PRICE:** INEXPENSIVE

You probably think there can be nothing at all romantic about eleventh- and twelfth-century religious tapestries and frescos, bas- and high-relief depictions of the Gospels, and the like. Well, think again. The Cloisters is the medieval branch of the Metropolitan Museum of Art, and the building itself was assembled from the very stones of several European monasteries. Wander around and see if there isn't a special place just waiting for you to duck into and kiss!

If the interior still seems too austere and religious for your romantic tastes, then do what we did. After paying, walk directly away from the admissions desk and past the walls of frescos; straight ahead is a chapel guarded, significantly, by a stone king and queen and several seated Old Testament figures. Just inside the chapel, make a left and follow the sign that says West Terrace to a dark and ominous-looking oak door, and then out onto the walled terrace that feels like a castle buttress. Here you can admire a wonderful view of the Hudson River, the New Jersey Palisades, and the George Washington Bridge in the distance.

To get to the Cloisters take the A train and get off at 190th. Turn right as you exit the station. From here you can take any of three paths to the Cloisters (you can see the bell tower straight ahead). If you take the steps down then follow the higher path, forgoing the second set of steps will take you closer to street level, you will pass through a short tunnel and climb another set of steps. A small stone cottage sits at the top of this stairway, and inside is the Fort Tryon Park Café (212-923-2233), a good place to return to for a sandwich and tea after taking in the Cloisters. The café is open Tuesday through Sunday, 11:00 A.M. to 5:00 P.M. for lunch, and 5:30 P.M. to 11:00 P.M. for dinner.

There is something about Fort Tryon Park, which surrounds the Cloisters, that makes it different from all other Manhattan parks. It's as if the city had set off the area as a park and then left it alone, did not try to "improve" on it. Hence, though it is a city park, it feels more natural, a bit more like being in a forest—a medieval forest if you're just returning from the Cloisters.

Of course, as with all city parks, one must be cautious. But if you stick to the clearly well-trodden paths, the main routes, you'll be fine. Don't let anything spoil your adventurous romanticism.

Coney Island Boardwalk

ADDRESS: END OF STILLWELL AVENUE, BROOKLYN, NY ♥
DIRECTIONS: BY SUBWAY, B, D, F, N TRAIN TO STILLWELL AVENUE

It's tacky and honky tonk, but if you're in the mood for low-rent romance, this has always been the spot. Earlier in the century, during an era of stricter social mores, many couples had their first physical contact on a ride in Steeplechase Park. That's gone, but you can still take a trip on two historic rides: the Wonder Wheel and the Cyclone. The Wonder Wheel, an anonymous Ferris Wheel saved from the 1939 World's Fair, affords a panoramic view of New York when you're stopped at the top. On a clear day, you can see from the Atlantic Ocean to the still-inspiring New York skyline. There are two types of cabs: stationary and swinging. On a windy day, with the ocean below, only the most adventurous of lovers will choose the latter.

Later on, try to get a front seat on one of the world's original roller coasters, the Cyclone. Its steep drops and speed will make you feel as if you'll go soaring into the Atlantic a few yards away, and you'll definitely end the ride clinging tightly to your partner. The exhilaration of the rides and the ocean air may stimulate your appetite, so take a left turn on Surf Avenue as you exit the Cyclone, and a short walk will lead you to the original Nathan's. Load up on French fries, hamburgers, and hot dogs. Walk one block to the boardwalk and enjoy your picnic lunch on one of the many benches overlooking the ocean. It probably will be too crowded for you to reenact the Burt Lancaster–Deborah Kerr scene in *From Here to Eternity* where they make love on the shore as waves crash over them (not at Coney Island, by the way), but if you're inspired, go ahead—the thousands of other couples making out nearby won't care. Even if you just feed the delicious, greasy French fries to one another, you'll still be having a classic lover's lunch.

Afterwards, stroll on the pier, where you can observe the catches of the day of the many fishermen as the sun sets over the ocean. If you're there during the fall or winter months, a skate in the *Abe Stark Skating Rink* (Surf Avenue and West 19th Street) would be a fun way to spend the evening. When it's not being used for various competitions, the rink is open for general skating, and many couples use it to practice their dance moves. Call for prices and schedule (718-946-3135).

$\mathcal{D}$ivine Bar

ADDRESS: 244 EAST 51ST STREET, NEW YORK, NY 10022 (BETWEEN SECOND AND THIRD AVENUE) ♥ **PHONE:** 212-319-WINE ♥ **HOURS:** WEEKDAYS OPEN AT 5:00 P.M.; SATURDAY AND SUNDAY OPEN AT 7:00 P.M. ♥ SUNDAY LIVE MUSIC STARTING AT 8:30 P.M.; NO COVER ♥ NO RESERVATIONS TAKEN ♥ **PRICE:** MODERATE

You guessed it! It's divine. It truly is. Enter through a crowded bar of beautiful businesspeople and ascend the stairs to romance. The first room you'll come to welcomes you with several comfortable couches and chairs and a blazing fireplace in colder weather. But you'll probably want to continue to the front room, where the two of you can have a quieter conversation. This room, too, has several seating options. Of course, we recommend the couch over the chairs. If you're hungry, the tapas are not to be missed and serve nicely as a delicious and filling supper. The food menu includes such things as potato pancakes with applesauce and baked brie, and desserts like white chocolate bread pudding in caramel, which is heavenly. The wine and beer menu is huge but reader-friendly. Try ordering a taste of several wines. The waitress will bring your selections in fine goblets, each sitting on a circle on a mat, identifying the wines by number. Take turns sharing the goblets, describing the taste, choosing your favorites, and guessing which is which. Out front in warmer weather is a cute little second-floor terrace. But be warned that the Divine Bar can get intensely loud and crowded. Call ahead to be sure you won't be spending your evening on line on the sidewalk. Early evening on Monday, Tuesday, or Wednesday or anytime on Sunday are the best times to try your luck.

In the warmer months take a stroll west on 51st Street. Cross the street and spend some time in *Greenacre Park*, a tiny concrete park with a huge waterfall, shady trees, happy birds, and dozens of places to sit and kiss and gaze into each other's eyes. You can't see it from the street, but when you enter you will find a little snack bar where you can buy a light lunch and lemonade. Avoid lunchtime, though, unless you want to get lost in the crowd. The park is closed at night and in the winter.

Hobart Beach, Eatons Neck, Long Island

There are easier, faster, and more direct routes to Hobart Beach than the one I'm about to give you, but this is my favorite because it passes through three of my favorite North Shore towns: *Cold Spring Harbor*, *Huntington*, and *Northport*. The beauty of this trip will be found as much in the driving as in the arrival. Before you start out, find Asharoken and Hobart Beach on the map. (Note that Hobart Beach is a private town beach and is only open to the public in a limited way during the peak hours of the high season.) Asharoken looks like a cap on a head with a long neck directly over the center of Long Island.

Try to get an early start for this trip. From the Long Island Expressway, take exit 43 North onto South Oyster Bay Road for a few miles. Turn right on Cold Spring Road and make a quick left, following the sign to stay on Cold Spring Road. At the end, it merges with 25A East, which you should take right into the town of Cold Spring Harbor. Spend as long as you like in Cold Spring Harbor, popping into the many antique and craft shops, ice cream parlors, and cafés. Surely, you'll spend some time gazing out over the harbor from the adorable *Cow Park* in the center of town. We recommend an informal, less expensive dinner in Northport, but if you can't hold out much longer and you're in the mood for a formal meal in a restaurant overlooking the harbor, you might consider dining in the *Inn on the Harbor* (very expensive; 105 Harbor Road, Cold

Spring Harbor, NY 11724; 631-367-3166). Or just get something to tide you over at the *Trattoria Grasso Due* (134 Main Street, Cold Spring Harbor, NY 11724; 631-367-6060).

When you're ready to move on, continue on 25A East through Huntington, which has more of a serious and sophisticated downtown shopping Main Street. If you're book lovers, you may want to spend some time in *Book Revue* (313 New York Avenue, Huntington, NY 11743; 631-271-1442) reading books together or listening to an author speak. It's my favorite independent bookstore on Long Island. Don't get too lost there, though, or you'll miss Northport and Hobart Beach. Soon after 25A becomes Fort Salonga Road, turn left on Woodbine Avenue, where the sign points to the village dock in Northport. Now you have a decision to make — whether to stay in Northport awhile and then go to Hobart Beach, or to go to Hobart Beach and then return to Northport for dinner. We suggest the latter.

To get to Hobart Beach, turn right on Northport's quaint New England–like Main Street past quaint shops like Jones Drug Store and the Northport Sweet Shop (remember, you'll be coming back). Then turn left at the church onto Ocean Avenue to the end. Turn left onto Eatons Neck Road and enjoy slowly the intriguing, almost surreal ride past pretty beaches, sprawling mansions, and breezy beach houses as you take the winding road almost to the end, where you'll see the sign for the town beach. Hobart Beach (open 8:30 A.M. to dusk) is a long spit of sandy beach that points south over the water to Huntington Beach and protects tiny Northport Bay, dividing it from Huntington Bay. Walk hand in hand as far south along the beach as your bare feet will take you and, weather permitting, enjoy a cool dip in the water. It's a slender beach with water on both sides, divided down the middle by a tern and plover nesting area, which must not be disturbed, as plovers are endangered (plovers are sweet and attractive birds, and we hope you'll be lucky enough to see some). On one side is the sleepy harbor filled with boats; on the other is a view of Lloyd Neck and Connecticut beyond. Hobart Beach is the perfect place to see the sunset unencumbered to the west.

When you start to get hungry, wend your way back to Northport. Directly across from the village dock is the restaurant we always head for. *Sea Shanty* (moderate; 14 Woodbine Avenue, Northport, NY 11768; 631-261-8538) is exactly as glamorous as the name implies, but it fits the bill. Something about a day at the beach makes you crave seafood in a tiny, family-style restaurant with wagon-wheel chandeliers, doesn't it? With only 10 tables, somehow it doesn't seem cramped. Salads, sandwiches, and fish and chips are available all day. Chowder, steamed clams, stuffed flounder—the food is so fresh and good, and there's not a better bargain to be had anywhere. It's packed on summer weekends, and no reservations are accepted. Sea Shanty is open for lunch and dinner seven days all year round.

Walk out to the end of the village dock while you're waiting for your table or after your meal. There are benches under a little gazebo at the end of the pier. If it's chilly, curl up together for warmth and watch the sailboats come in or the sun set. When you get home after this day's excursion, a good night's sleep is almost guaranteed.

$\mathcal{I}$l Tinello

ADDRESS: 16 WEST 56TH STREET, NEW YORK, NY 10019 (BETWEEN FIFTH AND SIXTH AVENUES) ♥ **PHONE:** 212-245-4388 ♥ **HOURS:** MONDAY THROUGH FRIDAY NOON TO 3:00 P.M. AND 5:00 P.M. TO 10:30 P.M.; SATURDAY 5:00 P.M. TO 10:30 P.M.; CLOSED SUNDAYS IN THE SUMMER ♥ **PRICE:** EXPENSIVE

This is an expensive Italian restaurant that I can't resist going back to again and again. Il Tinello exudes grace and hospitality with true, sophisticated Italian flair, and the food and service are as good as any you'll find in Tuscany.

The owner, Mario, will greet you warmly and usher you to the best available table. If you've been there before, he'll probably remember you and treat you like an old friend, which will definitely impress your date. Your chair will be drawn back for you and the Italian-speaking waiter will guide you with a flourish of his hand and the all-purpose Italian word, *prego*. Your water glass will be filled immediately, wines will be suggested, and before long, the most luscious-looking antipasto cart will arrive, and you'll enjoy hearing it and the many specials of the day described in great detail. Incredibly, the service is perfectly attentive without being intrusive.

The chef will prepare for you any conceivable Italian dish for which he has the ingredients, and you can rest assured it will be the best you ever had. Or choose from the huge menu such tempting entreés as scallopine monte blanco (veal with white wine, shallots, spinach, and mozzarella) or salmone Copa Santa (salmon with white wine, leeks, asparagus, and Dijon mustard).

The small room is delicately lit and filled with real-looking Renoir reproductions in fine gilt frames. The tables are well spaced, and people speak in comfortable, low tones. No matter how crowded the restaurant is, you'll feel alone with your date, and very, very special. Even though the restaurant is more simple than opulent, if I'm in the mood for a trip to Italy or for Italian food, I would choose Il Tinello for a Valentine's dinner or for sweetening up a plain Monday. Every couple should have a place to which to return.

$\mathcal{I}$nnisfree (Gardens)

ADDRESS: MILLBROOK, NY 12545 ♥ PHONE: 845-677-8000 ♥ HOURS: MAY 1 TO OCTOBER 20; CLOSED MONDAY AND TUESDAY EXCEPT LEGAL HOLIDAYS; OPEN WEDNESDAY, THURSDAY AND FRIDAY 10:00 A.M. TO 4:00 P.M; OPEN SATURDAY, SUNDAY, AND LEGAL HOLI-DAYS 11:00 A.M. TO 5:00 P.M. ♥ DIRECTIONS: FROM THE TACONIC PARKWAY, TAKE ROUTE 44 EAST ABOUT TWO MILES. AT COPPERFIELD'S RESTAURANT TURN RIGHT ON SOUTH ROAD AND RIGHT ON TYRREL ROAD. FOLLOW SIGNS TO INNISFREE. ♥ PRICE: INEXPENSIVE

North of New York City lie some of the prettiest mountains and lakes in the Northeast. Early in the twentieth century, some of the most desirable properties were bought by successful industrialists for their own private estates. Many of their mansions and gardens are now being opened for public use, to the advantage of those looking for romantic getaways.

Seventy miles from Manhattan is Innisfree, which was the private garden of Walter and Marion Beck. Influenced by the style of Chinese gardens and ancient Chinese paintings, Walter Beck invented the "cup garden." Using only American flora, fauna, and rocks, Mr. Beck created a series of 34 cup gardens surrounding a blissfully serene glacial lake. The different gardens contain varied combinations of streams, waterfalls, terraces, lotus pools, rocks, and plants. Each site is invisibly set off as if in a "cup" so it can be enjoyed in its own secluded area, perfect for a romantic interlude.

Walk counterclockwise around the entire lake and see all 34. There are benches and chairs to sit on, terraces to climb, and views to take in. Walk up steps, over bridges, under arches, beside walls, around ponds. Stop whenever you see something that interests you: a frog on a lily pad, a turtle in the water, a colorful flower, a tree with a particularly intriguing shape. You'll see, for example, a mist fountain spraying fine water particles into the air. The gentle gurgling of the lip waterfall in a meditative setting is sure to inspire a kiss. There is a bat house where, during certain times of the year, you can see the bats resting upside down. Innisfree is sure to take the city out of you in a hurry.

There's only one picnic area near the parking lot. If you would rather eat indoors, take Route 44 on your way back to the Taconic and stop in the strip mall at *Happy Days Restaurant and Malt Shoppe* (inexpensive; Route 44 Washington Hollow Plaza, Millbrook, NY 12578; 845-677-6244). As the name implies, the restaurant is a throwback to the 1950s. The walls and shelves are filled with pictures and statues of Marilyn Monroe, Elvis Presley, James Dean, and the Brooklyn Dodgers. Along with the burgers, fries, and sandwiches, you can sample the best egg creams north of Brooklyn. A chocolate malted is required for those not worried about their waistlines.

Early autumn is a beautiful time to drive on the Taconic, because of the many maple trees in the region. The red color mixed in with the yellow and orange tints of fall make for a truly romantic drive on a bright day.

Jamaica Bay Wildlife Refuge

ADDRESS: CROSS BAY BOULEVARD, QUEENS, NY ♥ **PHONE:** 718-318-4340 ♥ **HOURS:** REFUGE TRAILS ARE OPEN DAILY FROM SUNRISE TO SUNSET. THE VISITOR CENTER AND PARKING LOTS ARE OPEN EVERY DAY (EXCEPT THANKSGIVING, CHRISTMAS, AND NEW YEAR'S DAY) FROM 8:30 A.M. TO 5:00 P.M. ♥ **DIRECTIONS:** DRIVING, TAKE THE BELT PARKWAY TO EXIT 17 SOUTH (CROSS BAY BOULEVARD). ONE AND A HALF MILES PAST THE NORTH CHANNEL BRIDGE, TURN RIGHT INTO THE REFUGE. IF, LIKE MANY NEW YORKERS, YOU DO NOT HAVE A CAR, YOU CAN TAKE THE A TRAIN ON THE IND SUBWAY LINE TO THE BROAD CHANNEL STATION. AFTER EXITING, WALK WEST TO CROSS BAY BOULEVARD AND TURN RIGHT, GOING NORTH ABOUT ONE AND A HALF MILES TO THE ENTRANCE.

Jamaica Bay is a body of water between Kennedy Airport and Rockaway Beach in Queens. When the government realized that 325 different species of birds use the islands in the bay as a place to feed and nest, they decided to preserve the area in its natural state. And that was the luckiest thing for nature-lovers—and other lovers, too. You can see New York City and the Kennedy Airport control tower from certain spots at the Refuge—the view is ethereal and surreal, like a mirage. Get some binoculars and become bird-watchers together.

Start in the visitors' center, where you can pick up a map and permit for the day's exploration. Stroll through the South Garden, observing the flora and fauna. You will find some little nooks and blinds along the many trails for nature watching, and hopefully nobody will notice if you do a little smooching, too. The plants attract many types of butterflies, with the monarch being the most common, and you'll be ready to swear that they're following you.

Next, stroll along the main pathway called the West Loop Trail. It's one and three-quarter miles of wavy brush, red marshland, lush woodland, and fields filled with wildlife surrounding the West Pond. Keep your binoculars handy, as herons, geese, and egrets can be spotted at any time. Spring and fall are the best times to see birds migrating. Along the trail are several backless benches for relaxing, comparing notes, and taking it all in at the slowest possible pace. Fall, of course, is the best time to watch the foliage change color, but the Refuge provides a year-round haven for weary souls.

Whether or not you have an interest in amphibians, detour off the main trail for the terrapin nesting area, where you will be able to see where turtles start their lives and secure a little extra privacy for yourselves. On your left is a small beach that you're not supposed to walk on, but we saw a young couple there taking advantage of a semi-secluded spot (they obviously thought it was fully secluded). Further up the trail is an open area with views of the bay. It's a strange feeling to spot the New York skyline in the distance while still feeling a million miles away. Before returning to the visitors' center, take some of the hidden paths that comprise the North Garden.

If you've worked up an appetite or thirst from all the walking or are in the mood for a cocktail, on your exit from the Refuge continue south on Cross Bay Boulevard over the bridge into Rockaway. At 377 Beach 92nd Street is a restaurant hidden behind a McDonald's with no sign marking it. Walk through the recessed wooden gate to the left of the McDonald's and through the door into the *Pier 92 Restaurant* (moderately priced). It has a large terrace looking out onto the bridge and across to the refuge and the airport. It's open every day except Monday for lunch and dinner. Sit on the terrace, weather permitting, or inside where the décor is rustic. In the winter, sit beside the fire. The restaurant serves good American and Continental food with a German influence (steaks and chops, lobster and Sauerbraten). The phone number is 718-945-2200.

Jezebel

ADDRESS: 630 NINTH AVENUE, NEW YORK, NY 10036 (AT 45TH STREET) ♥ PHONE: 212-582-1045 ♥ HOURS: MONDAY TO FRIDAY NOON TO 3:00 P.M. AND 5:30 P.M. TO 10:00 P.M.; FRIDAY NOON TO 3:00 P.M. AND 5:30 P.M. TO 11:00 P.M.; SATURDAY 5:30 P.M. TO 11:30 P.M.; CLOSED SUNDAY ♥ PRICE: EXPENSIVE

When you first see the nondescript exterior of Jezebel (we walked by it twice before we noticed the modest brass nameplate on the door), it's hard to imagine that inside is a world reminiscent of a New Orleans–style bordello dripping with charm and romance. The lush plants that surround the small, lace-draped tables provide a setting for intimacy within a generously proportioned room. Tables for larger parties invite diners to sit on porch swings. A meal here is focused on relaxation, southern-style. So slow down and sit a spell! (Don't take your shoes off, though.)

The food and service are abundant with southern flavor; there are recognizable favorites like fried chicken and mashed potatoes. If you make your reservations late enough in the evening, you'll be able to enjoy your meal to live jazz. For a romantic southern setting in the midst of Manhattan, there's nothing like Jezebel.

We would suggest that Jezebel is the ideal place to start a weekday of theater, fine food, and strolling about. What better excuse for playing hooky from work than romance? Take off a weekday and meet for lunch at Jezebel, then head east to the *TKTS booth* at 47th and Broadway, where same-day tickets to shows go for 25 to 50 percent off. Most matinee shows start at 3:00 P.M.

And after the theater? Something exotic, classy, and festive? Try *Chez Josephine* (expensive; 414 West 42nd Street, New York, NY 10036, between Ninth and Tenth Avenues; 212-594-1925), a glamorous yet unpretentious French bistro, romantic and slightly bawdy, and truly "theatrical." This cabaret-like restaurant is run by Jean-Claude Baker, one of the many adopted children of the legendary Josephine Baker. Musicians play nightly, and Broadway stars and opera divas often sing at the piano.

Chez Josephine is open for dinner from 5:00 P.M. until 1:00 A.M.; the entreés are moderate to expensive. Chez Josephine is the perfect finale to a day of romantic fantasy: from a bordello in the Crescent City, to the illusion of the proscenium arch, to Gay Paris.

La Lanterna di Vittorio, "The Fireside Caffe"

ADDRESS: 129 MacDougal Street, New York, NY 10012 (just south of Washington Square Park) ♥ **Phone:** 212-529-5945 ♥ **Hours:** Open seven days 10:00 a.m. to 3:00 a.m. ♥ **Price:** Inexpensive

Located right near Washington Square Park, La Lanterna di Vittorio is the ultimate West Village café, the ideal place to feed each other Italian ricotta cheesecake or tartufo and other gelati desserts, sip cappuccinos with amaretto and whipped cream, and while away the afternoon. There are two working fireplaces, one upstairs and one down. Several genuine suits of armor point the way to the downstairs bar/café. Desserts, coffees and teas, and other beverages—such as 20 flavors of frozen granita—dominate the menu, but there is a fine selection of Italian-style sandwiches (panini), soups, and salads as well. The upstairs has an old-time soda fountain feel, while the downstairs is darker and looks more like a speakeasy. There are many, many casual cafés in

Greenwich Village, but this is my favorite and, I believe, the one most conducive to romantic feelings.

Either beforehand, to work up an appetite, or afterwards, to work off the chocolate mousse cake, the thing to do is stroll—north through Washington Square Park and along the charming Washington Mews (between University Place and Fifth Avenue), continuing east on Eighth Street (which becomes St. Mark's Place) to the East Village or, my preference, south again to Bleecker Street and all around the West Village—or even further south past Houston Street to Soho. Listen to street musicians, stop in shops and galleries, discuss your favorite New York places with tourists and friendly New Yorkers, and keep walking until you simply must stop and get yourself another couple of cappuccinos.

$\mathcal{L}$a Maison

BED & BREAKFAST ♥ ADDRESS: 404 JERSEY AVENUE, SPRING LAKE, NJ 07762 ♥ PHONE: 800-276-2088 ♥ CALL FOR DIRECTIONS BY CAR OR TRAIN OR REFER TO LA MAISON'S WEB SITE, WWW.LAMAISONINN.COM ♥ PRICE: EXPENSIVE

It's surprising for those who crack "Jersey jokes," but the New Jersey coast offers some of the prettiest stretches of shoreline in the Northeast. The towns along the Atlantic Ocean are popular weekend getaways, and one of these resort areas is Spring Lake. In the center of the town is the actual lake, Spring Lake, which is surrounded by a park filled with trees and flowers and paths. There are two arched bridges over the lake, made for biking and strolling, and you'll often see a bridal party posing for photographs on one of them. Bike-ride around the main street and you'll see many of the old Victorian mansions and hotels. The most romantic is a bed and breakfast called La Maison, originally built circa 1870 as a hostelry for traveling peddlers and craftsmen. It's the oldest inn in Spring Lake.

The proprietor's interest in French culture permeates the house. The rooms have a rosy and cheerful décor throughout; entering one is like stepping into an Impressionist painting. There are many Louis Phillippe–style antiques, and the rooms have either French sleigh or quarter beds. The King Carlos Room (expensive) is the best choice in the main house. The inn's sitting room is comfortable and inviting, with wine and cheese served between 5:30 and 7:30 P.M. If you would like to sit outside on a warm summer evening, you can take advantage of the porch that surrounds the house. For couples who would like a bit more privacy, La Petite Maison, a little cottage in back, is also a good choice. It has a tiny, hidden sleeping alcove behind curtains, wood floors, and a little screened porch with a soft couch. Breakfast is a feast for the eyes as well as the taste buds, and if you're in La Petite Maison, they'll bring the breakfast to the cottage and set it up for you on the porch.

You may want to work off that huge breakfast. Ask for a pool pass, a beach/pool pass, or a health club pass to one of the best health clubs in New Jersey, the Atlantic Club (1904 Atlantic Avenue, Manasquam, NJ 98736; 732-223-2100). Or grab one of the dirt bikes from the driveway and ride around the town, around the lake, by the beach, past the Victorian homes, to the shops.

At some point, to your great surprise, you're going to be hungry again for dinner. From La Maison, the proprietor will give you directions to *Red's Lobster Pot Restaurant* (moderately priced) at Red's Lobster Dock (57 Inlet Drive, Point Pleasant Beach, NJ 08742; 732-295-6622). This is a very casual, rustic sea shanty sort of place with the most excellent fresh seafood imaginable. The problem is everybody in the area knows about it, and there are only 19 tables. They don't take reservations, but the good news is you can sit outside at booths on the porch and stuff yourself with shrimp, Alaskan crabs, clams and oysters from Red's Lobster Dock kiosk. Watch the fishing boats come and go and the sun set over the inlet. Red's Lobster Pot is open for lunch and dinner, 11:00 A.M. to 9:00 P.M., and Sunday from noon to 9:00 P.M. It's closed Tuesday and November through March. Come during the week if you don't want to wait. BYOB.

$\mathcal{L}$e Refuge Inn

ADDRESS: 620 CITY ISLAND AVENUE, CITY ISLAND, BRONX, NY 10464 ♥ PHONE: 718-885-2478 ♥ HOURS: OPEN FOR DINNER EVERY NIGHT EXCEPT MONDAY AND TUESDAY

If you really press me, this is it: my number one favorite romantic dinner date in New York City. Whether you go for the bed and breakfast (moderately priced) or just for dinner, you'll swear you've been magically transported from New York City—the Bronx no less—to the French countryside. Right after you enter City Island, on the left, is an understated nineteenth-century sea captain's house, but you probably won't notice it until you enter the gate. On top of the tall layer-cake Victorian house, you'll see the widow's walk where the captain's wife may have spent many a lonely evening eagerly watching for the return of her beloved. Luckily for you, you can take your beloved with you. At this writing, the widow's walk is being renovated to serve as a deck with a year-round hot tub for inn guests. But that's only a hint of the pleasures that await you at Le Refuge Inn.

If you come just for dinner (very expensive), expect that your charming host Pierre will prepare for you his cuisine du coeur, a delectable three-course, French prix fixe dinner, which, considering the bounty and quality, is very reasonable by New York standards. Savor some escargots and *canard aux figues* (duck with fresh figs) as you sip wine at your candlelit table for two. The entire inn is warmly decorated in the French country style with authentic French antiques.

And your date doesn't have to end with dinner. As you wipe the last remnants of *gateau soufflé au chocolat* (chocolate cake) from each other's lips, you may want to discuss spending the night at one of the inn's charming rooms. There are seven bedrooms and three suites, each uniquely decorated with French antiques. Some rooms are modest, with shared baths, but still very comfortable and beautiful. Our favorite overnight choice is the cottage behind the main house. Inside is a comfortable living area featuring a Steinway baby grand piano and a French country kitchen. Stairs lead up to the bedroom and bath.

In the morning, wake up to croissants and coffee in the dining room, on the inn's back porch, or in your room. On Sunday mornings, Le Refuge Inn hosts classical concerts. The public is invited to attend for a fee; inn guests may attend free of charge.

Were it not for Le Refuge Inn, I would not call City Island a particularly romantic destination, but it's worth touring a little, especially if you are a boat lover. If you're there for the afternoon or for a second night, you'll probably be craving seafood. I recommend the lobster at The Harbor, 565 City Island Avenue, 718-885-1373 (Italian-American seafood; open every day for lunch and dinner). Sit by the window, and when you can take your eyes off each other, watch the many fishing boats outside.

Can't get to City Island? For a taste of Pierre's fine French cuisine, treat yourselves to a special evening in Manhattan at the rusticly elegant *Le Refuge Restaurant*, 166 East 82nd Street, 212-861-4505. Magnifique!

ℒiterary Love

BARNES & NOBLE, STRAND RARE BOOK ROOM, AND PAGEANT RESTAURANT AND LOUNGE

Can you be lovers and also be book lovers? The answer, of course, is "Yes yes I will yes" (James Joyce, *Ulysses*). Start by attending a reading or by browsing through the *Barnes & Noble* bookstore at Union Square (33 East 17th Street, New York, NY 10003, between Broadway and Park Avenue South; 212-253-0810). We like this particular B&N because it's on four levels and you get a great view of Union Square Park through the windows. Meander through the park, and if it's Monday, Wednesday, Friday, or Saturday before 6:00 P.M., you'll catch the *Greenmarket*, where you can buy a muffin, flower, or vegetable as an offering of your love—"My vegetable love should grow / Vaster than empires, and more slow" (Andrew Marvell, "To His Coy Mistress"). That wasn't really what Marvell meant, but we liked the sound of it, anyway.

Amble down Broadway to the *Strand*, but don't go into the main bustle of used-book anarchy at 828 Broadway (212-473-1452); instead, enter next door at 826 Broadway, which looks like an office building entrance. Ride to the third floor and visit the fabled *Strand Rare Book Room* (open daily from 9:30 A.M. to 6:30 P.M.). Rare first editions are found here. Even some of the staff has a literary pedigree: rare bookroom manager Craig Anderson's father was Maxwell Anderson, who wrote *High Tor*, always a staple of the *New York Times* crossword puzzle. Art books, fiction, poetry—whatever suits your tastes is here. A first edition of your lover's favorite author is one of the most loving gifts you can give or receive. Wander into a corner stack; maybe sneak a kiss when the rare book room guys aren't watching.

Now it's time to eat and drink. So on to the *Pageant Restaurant and Lounge* (inexpensive; 109 East Ninth Street, New York, NY 10003, between Third and Fourth

Avenues; 212-529-5333; call for hours), a restaurant
named after the former bookstore on its site. Pageant's
austere décor of honey-toned woods and golden-colored
textured walls is a far cry from the messy bookshop it
once was. (Get a glimpse of it in Woody Allen's movie
Hannah and Her Sisters, when Woody and Barbara
Hershey browse outside.) Entreés range from hearty
sandwiches to filet mignon. Now go home and read to
each other before you go to bed.

Lower East Side

Are Ludlow Street and the Lower East Side really
romantic? No, not in the classic sense of flowers and candlelight or moon-June. But it's young, funky, and fun.
And sometimes that's just what you need to jump-start
your love life. If your first thought at the mention of the
Lower East Side is "Isn't that where Grandma lived?"
then you may be a bit old for this excursion. Well, that's a
definite reason to do this fun little date.

Make the transition from the old Lower East Side to
the new with a stop at *Katz's Deli* (205 East Houston
Street, New York, NY 10002, at the corner of
Ludlow; 212-254-2246). No romantic atmosphere in
this fluorescent temple to meat, but the brisket sandwich will warm your heart (or clog its arteries),
and in *When Harry Met Sally*, Katz's was the site of

Sally's famous fake orgasm (remember "I'll have what she's having"?).

Turn right onto Ludlow Street and step into the long-standing hipster bar *Max Fish* (178 Ludlow Street, New York, NY 10002; 212-529-3959; open 5:30 P.M. until 4:00 A.M.). A sign boasts that the establishment has been there for 30 years. Teetotalers can step into the *Pink Pony* next door (176 Ludlow Street, New York, NY 10002; 212-253-1922; open 10:00 A.M. until 3:00 A.M. Sunday through Thursday and until 4:00 A.M. Fridays and Saturdays) for snacks, coffee drinks, or delicious ice cream. No one here remembers when JFK was shot or even life before answering machines (Remember when you used to wait by the phone in case your date called?). If you need a reminder of those times, or even if you were born after Nixon resigned, pay a visit to *Las Venus Twentieth-Century Pop Culture* (163 Ludlow Street, New York, NY 10002; 212-982-0608) for a dose of nostalgia. Vintage clothes and furniture are the thing here.

Now it's time for entertainment: walk down the block to Stanton Street and turn right. Head into *Arlene Grocery* (95 Stanton Street, New York, NY 10002, between Ludlow and Orchard; 212-358-1633). A nifty assortment of musicians such as Deni Bonet and Mission: On Mars plays here. There's music seven nights a week from 8:00 P.M. on, no cover, just stand around and buy drinks.

Maybe you'd like a detour to Latin America at this point. Enjoy Caribbean-inspired *Palador* (moderate, 161 Ludlow Street, New York, NY 10002; 212-473-3535).

The walls are done in lovely pastel colors, and the atmosphere is casual, hip, and lively.

Complete your urban adventure with a couple of souvenir tattoos at *Daredevil Studios* (174½ Ludlow Street, New York, NY 10002; 212-533-8303). If permanent skin pix are not your style, try this instead: on your way home, buy several boxes or little bags of Cracker Jacks. Remember how they used to come with those dinky little plastic prizes? Well, now, in the name of child safety, no doubt, it seems that the prize is not a plastic trinket, but a fake lick-on tattoo. Go home, stick on your faux skin art and challenge your paramour to find it.

March

ADDRESS: 405 EAST 58TH STREET, NEW YORK, NY 10022 (BETWEEN FIRST AVENUE AND SUTTON PLACE) ♥ PHONE: 212-754-6272 ♥ HOURS: MONDAY THROUGH SATURDAY 6:00 P.M. TO 11:00 P.M.; SUNDAY 6:00 P.M. TO 10:30 P.M. ♥ PRICE: VERY EXPENSIVE

March is a small and simple but elegant four-star restaurant located in a turn-of-the-century Upper East Side townhouse. March offers an unusual choice of menus. Everything is prix fixe, but you have four-through seven-course tasting menus (although the word "tasting" is misleading, since there is no regular menu from which you would be tasting, and the menus change daily).

What is most romantic about March? You can turn the whole show over to chef Wayne Nish and host Joseph Scalice. (Joseph is the one who more than likely met you at the door and welcomed you in, as he did us.) For the romantic couple who would rather hold hands than ponder the daily menu, chef Wayne will prepare a four- or seven-course meal "tailor-made" for two, complete with boutique wines paired by Joseph. (This "chef's menu" is expensive.) The cuisine is New American, although Wayne and Joe prefer the phrase "global cooking." We prefer to call it "cosmic."

The ambience at March is just what two people in love crave for special occasions: quiet, intimate, and splendid. There are three dining rooms with tables and many banquettes. The first is surrounded by nineteenth-century Florentine prints. The main dining room is "watched over" by a glorious Lalique chandelier; a wall of Chinese needlepoint tapestry faces a turn-of-the-century Parisian Chaltillon ceramic and wood carving. There are views of the 59th Street Bridge and the Roosevelt Island Tram from the new North dining room, the secluded Mezzanine, and the new rooftop terrace.

After dinner, stroll one block to one of the city's most charming "vest-pocket" parks, *Sutton Place Park* at the eastern end of 57th Street. There are quite a few benches ideal for snuggling, and the view of the East River and the Queensboro Bridge is most enticing. You can linger by the railing and watch the tugs plying the water. Best of all, you can stay in this little park until 1:00 A.M. if you are of two minds, or hearts.

$\mathcal{M}$onkey Bar

ADDRESS: Hotel Elysée, 60 East 54th Street, New York, NY 10022 (between Madison and Park Avenues) ♥ **PHONE:** 212-838-2600 ♥ **HOURS:** Monday through Friday noon to 2:15 p.m. and 5:30 p.m. to 10:45 p.m.; Saturday 5:30 p.m. to 10:45 p.m.; closed Sunday ♥ **DRESS:** jackets required ♥ **RESERVATIONS** recommended ♥ **PRICE:** Very expensive

Located in the charming Hotel Elysée, Monkey Bar is a terrific place to succumb to some jungle fever. Beautifully renovated in 1994, the bar is large and lively and is decorated with murals of—you guessed it—monkeys! You may want to avoid the high-powered crowd at the front bar (which may be hazy with cigar smoke) and wander in through the elegant lobby of the hotel. Once you enter the dining room, you're confronted with sophisticated furnishings in strong, vibrant colors with a subdued leaf motif. Large suede pillars dominate the tiered room. The table across from the entrance on the raised dais in the center of the room was featured in the movie *The Mirror Has Two Faces* and thus is the most requested. It isn't within conversation range of other tables, but it does put you on display, which may suit you if you're all dressed up and feeling show-offy. But for more secluded dining, choose one of the comfortable banquettes along the back wall. Then you can hold hands, sit close, and discreetly share food as you look out over the other beautiful people. Several young men have proposed marriage at the Monkey Bar. Getting ideas?

The menu is magnificently creative and changes with each season. Try to seduce your loved one with Nantucket oysters on the half shell with red wine shallot mignonette, followed by delicious Maine lobster with tarragon linguini, kohlrabi, and bouillabaisse. Not in the mood for seafood? The grilled beef tenderloin with chanterelle and black forest mushrooms, wilted spinach, and herbal red wine sauce is a popular dish, or try the Scottish venison with brussels sprouts, lingonberries, fromage blanc spaetzle, and white peppercorn sauce. Make sure you leave room for dessert because they have a fantastic chocolate soufflé.

If your appetite for food is satisfied but not your appetite for each other, stroll across the street to the small, adorable courtyard next to 535 Madison, the *Dillon Read Building*. In the summer, the waterfall is both beautiful and soothing. During the holiday season, the trees are lit with gorgeous white lights. It's a great place to continue that romantic mood, partake in a kiss or two, and perhaps get up to some monkey business.

*M*useum Music

At the three most popular New York City museums, on Friday and Saturday nights, you can feed your ears as well as your eyes. An early-evening trip to any one of these museums will be the perfect start to a romantic evening. On Friday and Saturday nights, the *Metropolitan Museum of Art* (inexpensive; Fifth Avenue and 82nd Street; 212-535-7710) is open until 8:45 P.M. You can hear chamber music echoing off the pillars of the Great Hall, where a quintet plays from 5:00 to 8:00 P.M. Pay the suggested donation and walk straight ahead up the main stairway to the second level. Before sitting down to enjoy the concert, you may want to sample some of the galleries. Turn left to the prints and photographic areas, or go straight ahead to see some of the most famous European paintings in the world. Or simply turn right past the Asian art and right again until you see the violin and cello players. Take a seat at one of the little cocktail tables, order glasses of wine, enjoy the candlelight, listen to the music, and with your partner, enter into your own private world. Weather permitting, find the elevator to the *Iris and B. Gerald Cantor Roof Garden*. It's especially lovely during sunset in summer. Put your arms around each other and gaze out over the trees of Central Park, which from that height looks like a lush green bed.

If architecture is more your interest, you can see one of the most famous examples of Frank Lloyd Wright's work, the *Solomon R. Guggenheim Museum* (1071 Fifth Avenue, New York, NY 10128, at 89th Street; 212-423-3500). It's open Friday and Saturday nights until 8:00 P.M. Friday is pay-what-you-wish night, and on Saturday the museum charges a single entrance fee. Take the elevator up to the top level, and as you make your way down the spiral ramp, you will be entertained with lively jazz music from around the world. Or sit at one of the tables in the museum rotunda on the ground level, imbibe cocktails and juices, munch on light refreshments, and direct your attention to the music and each other. The exciting WorldBeat Jazz rhythms from Brazilian or African or Middle Eastern bands booming throughout the great museum have led many couples to a night of dancing at clubs later on. Call for the schedule of bands as the type of music varies. Concerts are free with the price of admission.

In the summer, the *Museum of Modern Art** (MoMA, 11 West 53rd Street, New York, NY 10019; 212-708-9500) is my favorite museum music choice (concert info: 212-708-9491). In July and August the outdoor sculpture garden, itself one of New York's most romantic venues, is given over to "Music in the Garden under the Moon." Chamber music fills the garden from 6:00 to 8:30 P.M. on Friday and Saturday nights. Pay what you wish on Friday evenings; on Saturday evenings a single admission fee is charged. Arrive early enough to secure two chairs or a cozy spot on the ground against the back wall. The heavenly music can also be heard from the terrace of the museum's fine, albeit expensive, Italian restaurant *Sette* (expensive; enter through museum or after 5:00 P.M. at 12 West 54th Street; 212-708-9710). Sette is candlelit, with a nice, quiet bar, and it's decorated with Japanese flair in a quiet black, white, and gray. Sette features a jazz pianist on Thursday nights from 5:30 to 10:00 P.M. From September through June, MoMA's weekend concerts feature contemporary jazz artists and are held every Friday from 5:30 to 8:00 P.M. in the indoor garden café.

---

* During renovations, music at MoMA may be available at a different location until 2005. Please call ahead for information.

Yew York Botanical Garden

ADDRESS: 200TH STREET AND SOUTHERN BOULEVARD, BRONX, NEW YORK 10458 ♥ PHONE: 718-817-8700 ♥ HOURS: OPEN YEAR-ROUND TUESDAY THROUGH SUNDAY AND MONDAY HOLIDAYS; APRIL THROUGH OCTOBER: 10:00 A.M. TO 6:00 P.M.; NOVEMBER THROUGH MARCH: 10:00 A.M. TO 4:00 P.M. ♥ COMBINATION TICKETS AVAILABLE AND RECOMMENDED ♥ PRICE: INEXPENSIVE

To see flowers, summer is the best time to visit the 250-acre New York Botanical Garden, but it's actually stunning all year round, and in the off months you just may have it to yourselves.

Once you decide who is paying for the date and orient yourselves with maps, admission tickets, and other assorted paperwork, you'll be ready to relax. Here's your romantic itinerary: straight ahead of you inside the gate, you'll see the tram stop. Take the tram to the Snuff Mill, then walk north past the Snuff Mill on the path that takes you along the Bronx River through the "forest." If they're not lying, the Bronx River is the only freshwater river in New York City, and the 40-acre "forest" is "a remnant of the woodland that once covered New York, traversed by rustic paths" (Caution: you'll be talking like this yourselves by the time you leave the gardens). Except for the quiet hum of traffic, you are certain to forget that you're in New York City. We went on a beautiful summer Sunday and had this path completely to ourselves.

Stop to see the waterfall by Hester Bridge. It's picturesque from every angle. Return along

Magnolia Road, stopping in the various gardens. The Daylily Garden doesn't look like much from the road, but enter it and sit inside the carved-out shrubbery and just see if you can dare leave without a kiss (there's no way). Stop also at the Family Garden if there's time, but don't miss the Rose Garden when it's in full bloom because, after all, the rose is the flower of love. Pick up a fallen petal and feel its incomparable smoothness against your lover's skin. Breathe deeply from the most compelling blossoms (but watch those thorns). Then return to the tram at the Snuff Mill and finish the tour.

Before you leave the gardens, visit the Enid A. Haupt Conservatory, where you'll see thousands of brightly colored flowers and exotic plants. Whenever you walk under a tree, you have my permission to announce that it's mistletoe, and kiss.

Birds, waterfalls, roses, Italian ices. What more could two people want?

Nearby: Right across the street is the *Bronx Zoo Wildlife Conservation Park*. To some, the Bronx Zoo is the epitome of romance. To others, it's a place to take children. I'm of the former school. You decide for yourself.

New York City Hotel Roundup

You don't need a weekend reservation at New York's most glamorous hotels to enjoy the fine surroundings of their lounges and lobbies and the quiet nooks and crannies of their sitting areas. In fact, you'll fit right in with their nighttime crowd—all the out-of-town visitors dressed up for their big night out on the town—and you'll enjoy the fine ambience of these quiet, elegant destinations as much as if you were a registered guest. These places have been designed to be eye-catching, inviting, and illuminating, so choose your spot from the locations listed below and get ready to be welcomed—even if only for a few hours—to a place people from all over the world pay big bucks to call home for an evening or two.

At the *Plaza Hotel* (Fifth Avenue and 59th Street, New York, NY 10019; 212-759-3000), you'll find the world-renowned *Oak Room* (very expensive), the winner of the 1999 Five-Star Diamond Award. With its dark wood walls, its fantastic architecture, and its tiled floors, it captures the essence of a quiet, classy club. All around you, you'll see such elegant touches as topiaries, hand-carved crests, classic artwork, and gold brocade curtains to set the mood. The lighting, except for the overhead chandelier, is dim, and you'll be quietly comfortable in a private banquette over in the corner. In fact, couples lounge at these choice high-backed leather seats, lit from behind by their own private lamps, and the quiet chatter of the room is softened by the sounds of the live piano music playing over at the other side of the room. The Oak Room, with its dark motif, is quite welcoming to the cozy couple, and you'll find yourselves nestled into those comfy leather chairs for as long as they'll let you stay. The Oak Room is quite an upscale destination; jackets and ties are required, and the award-winning menu is steep in price. The Oak Room does have a prix fixe pre-theater menu which includes a choice of filet mignon, salmon, prime rib, and desserts that include tiramisu.

If you don't mind smoke and want to experience a less-expensive version in a more relaxed but equally cozy atmosphere, choose to step next door to the *Oak Bar*, another dark-wood gathering place with inviting leather banquettes and choice seats by the large windows overlooking Central Park. The lights here too are dim, and you'll be surrounded by happy couples who are just starting off their romantic evenings with a stop at one of the city's most famous attractions. If you're interested in sipping cognac and puffing on fancy cigars, you won't find a more compelling venue.

When you have polished off your bottle of wine, step out into the marble walkways of the Plaza Hotel and check out which theater tickets are being sold at the ticket center. If spending the bucks to go to the theater is not in your plans for the evening, or if you'd rather do something more romantic than sitting in the dark watching a show for three hours, then continue your foray through the Plaza. It in itself is quite an attraction. You can play Holly Golightly by window-shopping for all the fabulous, sparkling jewelry in the windows of Maurice Fine Jewelry, dreaming about the five-carat solitaire you'll someday wear on your left hand, or you can even stop in to try on the breathtaking emerald and diamond chokers. Such an imaginary shopping spree is a girl's dream come true, and your partner will love watching you pose in front of a mirror with a necklace that's worth more than the average house hanging around your neck. Next, stop at the chocolatier for a truffle or two. Feed each other your favorite chocolate-dipped fruit pieces, and grab a bag for munching in the cab.

As you continue on through the Plaza, you'll come upon the *Palm Court*, a virtual palace of white and gold décor that will remind you of an outdoor terrace in the islands. Palm trees punctuate the space here, and all that's missing is an open-air breeze. With the added attraction of the statuettes accenting the large mirrored windows, you'll feel as though you've been invited to appear in a segment of *Lifestyles of the Rich and Famous*, dining on the terrace of some publishing magnate's house. The soft-colored tables and comfy sea-foam and coral-colored chairs are set far apart for privacy, and the tables are lit by candles for an even warmer romantic glow. Delicate flowers add to the garden atmosphere.

If you and your sweetheart are game to try it, come to the Palm Court (very expensive) for afternoon tea or high tea. Afternoon tea is served at 3:45 P.M., and the menu includes English tea sandwiches, scones, and pastries accompanied by loose tea selections. For high tea, you can choose from caviar blinis, prosciutto and mozzarella, and loose tea. Sometimes this step out of the routine of the regular evening romantic dinner out is just the answer for the couple who have done everything. So try this elegant option. You'll enjoy your tea, served in delicate fine china, as you are seated next to society ladies in hats, elderly couples who have been in love since the dawn of time, and other happy couples who've come to the Plaza's Palm Court for an afternoon delight. Listen to the soft romantic music playing in the background, and share a moment with the royalty of England.

If afternoon tea is too "ladies' garden club" for you or for your partner, then head further down the white marbled Plaza Hotel hallway to the *Oyster Bar*. Dimly lit, the Oyster Bar has a 1920s motif with period artwork on the walls, and with the easy jazz saxophone music playing on the sound system, you'll feel right at home as you take one of the choice, private seats by the etched-glass windows overlooking Central Park. All around you, couples drink their wine and suck down their oysters on the half shell. Through a glass window in the wall you'll see the chef at work cracking open the shells for you, and your mouth will water at the sight of all those crab claws. For the seafood lover—and the seafood sharer—the Oyster Bar is the quiet, cozy corner for your pre-evening start.

The Peninsula Hotel (700 Fifth Avenue; New York, NY 10019, on the corner of 55th Street; 212-956-2888) welcomes you with an impressive grand staircase at the entrance, beckoning you upstairs to two of its most romantic spots.

The Gotham Lounge is a casual, comfortable spot where the two of you can pick a two-seater table from among eclectic assortments. All of the table and chair arrangements are different, so you can choose from the gold brocade high-backed chairs or a low-slung comfy couch with a coffee table to hold your order. As you wait for your drinks, enjoy the conversation-starting artwork of book prints and the fresh floral arrangements on each table. The seats by the window are perfect for grabbing that quiet corner of solitude, and the unobtrusive staff will allow you to stay for hours.

On the other side of the hotel is the Peninsula's more formal gathering spot, where jackets are required. *Adrienne* is the name of this striking black-and-white eatery, and the well-set tables are spaced far apart to let you grab your own oasis. Along the back wall, you'll find a large black leather banquette, comfortable and cozy for your perfect situation. Set back here, you'll be far from the foot traffic of the other diners, and you can still hear the romantic sounds of the restaurant. A piano plays in the background as you sip your martini or champagne, and reflections of the sunset stream through the large half-circle windows overlooking Fifth Avenue.

Here, you'll be transported to romantic Paris, finding yourself in what might be a posh eatery on the Seine. Your French waiter's accent will tickle you, and you'll sample the fine cuisine from the menu. This is a quiet escape from the rest of the city, and indeed from the rest of the hotel, and you'll absorb the romantic mood as the dim lighting, the piano serenade, and the French wine inspire you to plan that getaway to Paris someday.

At the *St. Regis Hotel* (Two East 55th Street, New York, NY 10022, between Fifth and Madison Avenues; 212-753-4500), you'll find you've just entered a romantic country manse, finding rooms at every corner suitable for a tête-à-tête away from prying eyes and ears. First, you'll come to a lushly decorated private sitting room with a brocade couch and old English chairs, an ornate marble fireplace filled with romantic oversized flower arrangements, and a unique chandelier of a rose décor. If it's absolute privacy you want, grab the two red brocade chairs by the window overlooking Fifth Avenue, and sit for hours as you sip your wine and spend some quiet time together in what might remind you of the library of an old English manor house.

From here, you can hear the live harp or piano music coming from the nearby *Astor Court* (very expensive), named after the famous Astor family of New York City wealth and glamour. Astor Court is a lavish dining area, light in color and with romantic murals on the walls. The ceiling mural depicts blue sky with clouds, and you'll feel as if you're sitting beneath a clear blue sky no matter what the weather outside. The tables are spaced far apart and the chairs are so inviting, you'll never want to end your dining experience here, being looked down upon by the angels on the walls and serenaded by the harpist or pianist.

Even at afternoon high tea, during which society ladies dine wearing their designer hats, the lights are dimmed for a comfortable feel. You'll sip your tea from fine china, hearing all around you the upper-echelon clinking of tiny stirring spoons and the plunking of sugar cubes. Champagne corks pop in the background, as you'll notice happy couples all around you starting their day together with a unique and memorable tea service. At Astor Court, the afternoon tea includes tea sandwiches, scones, petits fours, and tea, while the champagne afternoon tea includes Perrier Jouet Champagne.

If you've missed afternoon tea, you can dine at Astor Court, or you can continue on through the white marbled hallway to the elegant *Lespinasse*. If you have ever toured a royal castle such as that of the late Princess Grace in Monaco, you'll be reminded of it when you look into this room. You'll feel as if the place is much too beautiful to enter—as if there should be a red velvet rope holding out all intruders. But the heavenly colored tan and light blue Lespinasse, with its high-domed ceilings, its original murals, and its too-large-for-reality floral centerpieces, will welcome you for an elegant, romantic dining experience, during which you'll become royalty yourselves as you slip into one of the private banquettes on the sides of the room. The spaciousness of the room is quite attractive, the lighting is dim, and romantic music plays to accompany your laughter and conversation. This is a warm atmosphere, accentuated by the notable service you'll receive—don't you just love it when a waiter keeps appearing to fill your water glass when you've barely finished a sip?—and you will add Lespinasse to the places to rave about to all your coupled friends. Jackets and ties are required for entrance to this palace on Fifth Avenue. Princess Grace would accept no less.

If you've forgotten your jacket, or if the prices at Lespinasse are too steep for you, cozy on in to the *King Cole Bar* next door, a dark, swanky cigar bar lined with an impressive, original, Old World–style mural of Old King Cole. Grab one of the dark leather banquettes around the edge of the bar—to stay away from that cigar smoke—and enjoy a fine after-dinner drink, such as a Grand Marnier, Scotch, or espresso. It's loud and chatty in here, so you'll have to sit next to your loved one and lean in close to have your conversation, but that kind of proximity makes hand-holding all the easier.

Outside the King Cole Bar you'll find another sitting area with couches and marble tables, where you can take an intimate seat by the window next to the piano. The light is a little brighter out here than in the King Cole bar, but it's still dim enough to set a romantic mood.

At the *New York Palace* (455 Madison Avenue, New York, NY 10022, between 50th and 51st Streets; 212-888-7000) you'll enter into a busy lobby area, but you'll be floored by the coral-colored marble columns and the grand, sweeping staircase. Again, the aptly named Palace is a rich atmosphere suitable for kings and queens, and you'll be quite welcome to grab a private table at one of the café areas for some quiet time alone. There are many tables here for chatting, with comfortable high-backed chairs that can be pulled together for a little closeness. Live piano music is always playing, and the enjoyable easy-listening tunes just might get you humming along— or your sweetheart can sing "your song" into your ear.

Upstairs, where the Palace's banquet halls are located, you'll find an even more private sitting area, with unique high-backed art deco couches and chairs set off to the side of a stately, coral-colored marble gas-heat fireplace and a matching water fountain. Elegant candelabras make the mood lighting perfect for your own refuge from the din below, or for a slow-dance to the piano music playing in the background, and you just might catch an excited bridal party making their grand entrance into a wedding reception. So stand aside, clap for the happy couple, and enjoy the same fine atmosphere that they chose for this perfect moment together.

One If by Land, Two If by Sea

ADDRESS: 17 BARROW STREET, NEW YORK, NY 10014 (BETWEEN
SEVENTH AVENUE SOUTH AND WEST FOURTH STREET) ♥ PHONE:
212-228-0822 ♥ HOURS: OPEN SEVEN DAYS 5:30 P.M. TO 11:30 P.M.
♥ PRICE: VERY EXPENSIVE

This French-American restaurant is located in Greenwich
Village, in the house where Aaron Burr once lived. Beef
Wellington is the specialty; the rest of the menu is superb,
but never mind the cuisine. The restaurant itself is brim-
ming over with romance, from the warmth of two well-
stoked fireplaces, to the sumptuous flower arrangements,
the attentive waiters, and the lilting piano music. (If
you're having an early dinner, before the pianist has
arrived, expect the lush sounds of Ravel and Debussy
over the sound system.) Warm, elegant, stately. A wonderful place to "pop the question."

If you're taking a taxi, and you have the time, forget
about having your driver drop you at the door. It's not
the easiest place to find if you've never been there
before. Instead, on a nice evening, plan to arrive anywhere around Sheridan Square, at Seventh Avenue and
Christopher Street, and take advantage of all those
quaint little West Village streets on either side of
Seventh Avenue. On a weekend night Sheridan
Square itself can get quite busy, but the side streets
(between Barrow and Greenwich Avenue on
either side of Seventh Avenue) are less busy and
are loaded with old New York charm. Just keep

in mind that Bleecker and West 4th Streets, which run east–west for most of their length, slowly turn north as you walk west; you could get disoriented if you're not paying attention.

When you're ready to go to the restaurant, wind your way back to Seventh Avenue where it intersects with Barrow and Bleecker. East of the avenue on Barrow, on the right-hand side of the street, you'll find One If by Land.

Palisades Interstate Park, NJ

PHONE: FORT LEE HISTORIC PARK: 201-461-1776; ENGLEWOOD BOAT BASIN: 201-894-9510; ALPINE BOAT BASIN: 201-768-9798; STATE LINE LOOKOUT STAND: 201-750-0465; BEAR MOUNTAIN: 845-786-2701
♥ DETAILED TRAIL MAPS AVAILABLE AT FORT LEE HISTORIC PARK, OR CONTACT THE NEW YORK–NEW JERSEY TRAIL CONFERENCE, GPO 2250, 232 MADISON AVENUE, NEW YORK, NY 10016 OR CALL 212-685-9699.

The scenic seven-mile Henry Hudson Drive we recommended begins at the Edgewater–Fort Lee border and ends at the Alpine Boat Basin. It is only open, weather permitting, from dawn to dusk, from the first Saturday in April to the last Sunday in October; the Ross Dock parking area only allows seasonal parking. Boat basins are open May through October, but the *Englewood Boat Basin* parking area (at exit 1) and the *Alpine Boat Basin* parking area (at exit 2) will afford you year-round access for fishing, hiking, and picnicking, and the Fort Lee

Historic Park (just south of the George Washington Bridge) is open all year, too.

At the end of the last ice age, glaciers cut a path through the mountains on the way to New York harbor. When this path filled in with water, the Hudson River was born. It is the dividing line between New York and New Jersey, and the natural beauty of its shores exists even today. Its breathtaking cliffs are called the Palisades, and the George Washington Bridge is the New Yorker's path over the Hudson into the Palisades of New Jersey.

When you leave the bridge, take the Palisades Interstate Parkway to exit 1 and turn left toward the water. If it's open, follow the sign onto Henry Hudson Drive and continue on this beautiful drive south past the first boat basin until you come to the parking lot at *Ross Dock*, which is the parking area closest to the George Washington Bridge. The parking lot at Ross Dock juts so far out into the water that from it you can look straight out under the middle of the George Washington Bridge. At high tide, the water at Ross Dock splashes over the wall at your feet.

Pick up a trail map as you enter the parking area. There are two trails available to you—the shore trail along the water and the trail at the top of the Palisades, marked by blue squares. The two trails are each 11 miles long and begin near the George Washington Bridge and end at the New York State line.

From Ross Dock, take the shore trail just a short distance south along the water to where it begins, and stand under the George Washington Bridge. Feel exhilarated by its power and majesty. See the Little Red Lighthouse, cute and nostalgic, beneath it. Continue a little further, to the boat launching area, and gaze out together at the New York skyline. Then decide whether you wish to walk further on or to set out by car for another boat basin.

For a small fee you may park at any of the boat basin parking areas. Get out and take a walk or have a picnic. Or bring your bicycles and see more. The *George Washington Bridge* is fun to walk or bicycle over. Take a few steps down to Fort Lee Historic Park, just south of the bridge, for views of the New York side of the Hudson or to pick up more detailed trail maps.

Alternatively, when coming off the George Washington Bridge, you can drive to exit 2, which is the Alpine Boat Basin. There you will find a more tranquil environment, with benches along the water, kayakers and boaters going by, people flying kites (you may want to bring one yourself). Or take the scenic Henry Hudson Drive the full six miles north to the Alpine Boat Basin parking area.

In the winter, it's great fun and beautifully scenic to go cross-country skiing at *State Line Lookout* (exit 3 from the Palisades Parkway). Or just take a winter walk and warm up with some steaming hot chocolate at the Lookout Inn.

The Parsonage

ADDRESS: 74 ARTHUR KILL ROAD, STATEN ISLAND, NY 10306
(CORNER OF CLARKE) ♥ **PHONE:** 718-351-7879 ♥ **HOURS:** OPEN
FOR DINNER SEVEN DAYS AT 5:00 P.M.; CLOSED MONDAYS IN SUMMER;
OPEN FOR PRIVATE PARTIES SATURDAY AND SUNDAY AFTERNOONS ♥
PRICE: MODERATE

The Parsonage is so named because in 1855 it was built as
the home of the minister of the Reformed Dutch Church of
Richmond Town. Now it's an award-winning restaurant
serving food that's worth traveling long distances for served
in a rapturous environment. The landmark wood-frame
home has been restored and is part of Historic Richmond
Town, which includes 27 historic buildings spanning three
centuries located on a hundred acres of open land.

The Parsonage is decorated with comfortable and
authentic-looking reproductions of circa-1855 furniture.
Each room of the small house serves as a separate dining
room, none with seating for more than 20 people. One
dining room may be reserved exclusively for a single party
of two, but to score that on a weekend you'll need to
reserve six months in advance. During the week, it's far
more obtainable. In all of the rooms, classical music
enhances the ambience and makes for even more privacy. On the windows are lace curtains, on the tables
candles, on the ceilings original but electrified chandeliers, on the walls marvelously ornate champagne-
and gold-colored wallpaper. Every detail conspires
to capture a romantic mood of days gone by. The

menu changes all the time, but from the escargot to the crusted pompano with figs and yellow oyster mushrooms to the chocolate cheesecake, you'll find the food to be exquisitely prepared and presented. Many a couple have gotten engaged and married in and around the Parsonage.

If you're a historically minded couple and you want to travel back in time together, arrive early in the day to stroll around *Historic Richmond Town* (inexpensive; 441 Clarke Avenue, Staten Island, NY 10306; 718-351-1611; a small admission fee is charged for the tour; it's free if you just want to stroll around the grounds). Walk through the 25 acres that have been restored so far. You'll see workman's shops, small factories, and curiosities such as train stations, a 1695 schoolhouse on its original site, and even an outhouse. Watch women weave and men make utensils out of tin (which you can buy). Stroll through an old general store and imagine what your life would be like together without dishwashers and TV sets.

Consider taking a drive after dinner to *South Beach Park*, which starts where Father Capodanno Boulevard meets Sand Lane. Stroll on the boardwalk and beach and watch the lights twinkle on the Verrazano-Narrows Bridge.

Piermont-on-the-Hudson and Nyack, NY

On a weekend that you want to get out of town but not really go away for the whole weekend, Piermont would be a great choice for an excursion. Just a couple of decades ago, Piermont was a rather unlovely industrial rivertown on the Hudson, home of the reclusive novelist William Gaddis. It had a couple of Italian restaurants more notable for their location—the docks, where sailors could anchor and then eat—than for their cuisine. It also had several boarded-up storefronts, and Woody Allen even used the main street in scenes from his movie *The Purple Rose of Cairo*, because it had that grim Depression feel. Gradually, the gentrifiers waved their magic wands. The cannery became condos; empty storefronts turned into galleries, craft stores, and antique shops; and food of a serious nature came to Piermont, now transformed into a rather chic little village just a few miles south of Nyack and renamed Piermont-on-the-Hudson.

It's an easy drive up on Route 9W or the Palisades Parkway, and if you're without a car like so many New Yorkers, just catch the number 9 bus at the George Washington Bridge Bus Terminal (itself still a very unlovely—albeit improving—place). Stroll down *Piermont Avenue* poking into little stores; then fall into the *Freelance Café and Wine Bar* (moderately priced; 506 Piermont Avenue, Piermont, NY 10968; 845-365-3250; no reservations taken, unfortunately). Entreés range from penne with portabello mushrooms and Courvoisier to soft-shell crabs tempura with wild watercress salad (seasonal, of course). Tightly packed but not-too-cramped tables flank the wine bar and don't offer the most romantic atmosphere around, but the food makes up for the crowding. For real romance, you've got to dress up and pay the price at neighboring *Xaviar's at Piermont* (very expensive; 506 Piermont Avenue, Piermont, NY 10968; 845-359-7007).

You must reserve well ahead for this most intimate of Piermont places. Meals here are elegant and astounding. The prix fixe menu or chef's tasting menu offer such delicacies as roast rack of American lamb for two with fresh rosemary and garlic flan (remember, if you want to kiss you have to both eat the garlic). Or try the grilled squab accompanied by barley risotto with apple and truffles. A tiny, classic room of white cloth-covered tables sparkling with candlelight, Xaviar's is a place for special occasions.

If your idea of fun is more casual and outdoorsy, it's great to rent bicycles in Piermont and ride through Piermont, Grandview, and Nyack, a round trip of 12 beautiful miles. *Piermont Bicycle Connection* (inexpensive; 215 Ash Street, Piermont, NY 10968; 845-365-0900; call for hours and prices) will rent bicycles for a few hours or a full day. You just need a driver's license and a credit card, and you can leave your car in an adjacent lot (or go by bus to Piermont). Pedal up Piermont Avenue to Grandview, where the avenue changes its name to River Road. On your left a cliff rises behind the distinctive houses that line the one street of this tiny hamlet. On your right the Hudson sparkles behind the beautiful houses. Keep riding until you get to Nyack. Follow the green bicycle-route lanes and continue onto South Broadway. A bicycle is the perfect vantage point from which to view the lovely large mansions on Broadway. Continue up Broadway through Upper Nyack, where the mansions are even more grand. (Here's where Rosie O'Donnell bought the old Helen Hayes house.) When you get to Nyack Beach State Park, if you still have the stamina, you can ride on the gravel path another six miles north to Haverstraw, enjoying the beautiful river view, and then turn around and pedal back to Piermont and take in a second dose of the view.

Even without the exertion of bicycling, you can find much to love in *Nyack*. The *Southern Comfort Restaurant* (expensive; Seven Main Street, Nyack, NY 10960; 845-353-1775) is the place for hearty food, such as baby back ribs served with side dishes like grits and collard greens. Located near the water in a beautiful Victorian house, the restaurant has a garden terrace where you can sit; or you can cuddle by the fireplace if it's wintertime.

Another pastime in Nyack is antiquing—there are many wonderful shops all along Broadway and Main Street. Or catch a play at the *Helen Hayes Performing Arts Center* (117 Main Street, Nyack, NY 10960; 845-358-6333; call ahead for reservations and details on what's playing).

$\mathcal{P}$ort Jervis and Upper Delaware River

For couples who love a scenic day in the car, the Port Jervis area is the perfect destination. Just 60 miles from New York City, it is a reasonable, albeit long, day trip—but oh, how much more lovely it is to wake up in a room overlooking a lake. Call ahead, for example, to the very clean and reasonable no-frills Fantasy Lake View Farm Resort, 149 Airport Road, Yulan, NY 12792, a half-hour drive north from Port Jervis (845-557-3550). A few savvy city-weary

Russian immigrants have made this their favorite country destination. Warning: some rooms have no air conditioning.

There are many ways to reach Port Jervis from New York, but we recommend Route 80 to Route 23 if you don't mind some lights and prefer antique shops to highway signs. If you're hungry, stop for a real-life taste of Mayberry at *Homer's* at Two East Main Street, Port Jervis, NY 12771 (845-956-1712). You can feast on home-style food very inexpensively. Then drive north on Route 97, which takes you along the Delaware River. Go at least as far as Hawks' Nest and stop along the road to view the spectacular panorama far below. If it's summer, you'll watch from an eagle's-eye view rafters, tubers, and canoers far below, floating lazily past the cliffs along the winding river. Speaking of eagles, it's very possible you'll see one or more fishing the river for its own meal.

If you're up for it, keep going. We know you'll agree that the dots that mark the scenic Route 97 on the map should be changed to huge circles with exclamation points. As you continue north on the winding mountain road, stop at the ranger station at *Pond Eddy* to cuddle a cat, chat with the amiable and helpful rangers, and take in the quiet deck view on the river, which is as calm as glass after the rafters go home at dusk. Pick up an armful of brochures that will help you further explore and appreciate the magnificent beauty of this region.

Truly adventurous couples will want to continue further north, as we did, to the Roebling Bridge, which is an adorable miniature of the famous Brooklyn Bridge and certainly an inspiring locale for stealing a kiss or two.

Raoul's

ADDRESS: 180 PRINCE STREET, NEW YORK, NY 10012 (AT SULLIVAN STREET) ♥ **PHONE:** 212-966-3518 ♥ **HOURS:** OPEN SEVEN DAYS 6:00 P.M. TO 2:00 A.M. ♥ **PRICE:** EXPENSIVE

You won't know there's a back room at Raoul's unless somebody tells you. You can't see it. There's no sign. But it's reservable, and that's where you'll want to go, even though it's the only part of the restaurant where smoking is allowed. (I'm sensitive to smoke and didn't find it a problem. Besides, I've seen people smoke in the front, too, without being asked to stop.)

You will be guided right through the cramped kitchen to get to it. A cook might nudge past you in his rush to save the *tourte chaud au chocolat*. No matter, that's part of the fun. Keep going. What you can expect to see when you get to "the garden room" is a small, candlelit solarium with one brick wall, many cozy corners, and banquettes for two. There's a view through the glass of a tiny, quirky garden with four tables, an umbrella, some flowers, and a cupid engaged in an activity that's usually considered private. You might choose to sit outside beside the cupid, even in a light rain shower.

There are many eccentric, mischievous touches that make Raoul's so enchanting. For example, the mural in the garden room looks normal at first—a view of New York with the Statue of Liberty and the beautiful skyline. But once your eyes adjust, you'll see that this New York includes the Eiffel Tower, as if to say that on a clear night, you can see all the way to Paris. (And you can. The fine French food would be worth coming for even if the décor at Raoul's were less than extraordinary.) Another thing you might miss, unless the cupid inspires you to visit the restroom—which is up the front spiral staircase—is the tarot card reader who sits outside the restroom just waiting to read your future if you will cross her palm.

Avoid the front room on the weekend unless you are lucky enough to score a booth. But if it's not crowded, the front room has some nice touches to recommend it, such as sexy pictures on the wall, and tin walls and ceiling.

Dress casual or dress up. Raoul's is a great choice for a special occasion or when you want to impress a special person. But let's keep this a secret between us, OK? It's hard enough to get a reservation here.

$\mathcal{R}$ockefeller Center

ADDRESS: Enter Rockefeller Center at Fifth Avenue between 49th and 50th Streets

Although Rockefeller Center is always crowded with businesspeople munching sandwiches on flower-lined benches and tourists snapping pictures of each other in front of the stunning architecture and plantings, there is always a peaceful and calming aura to this landmark that will make you and your date feel like you're the only two people there.

In winter, stroll through festive Rockefeller Center holding glove-clad hands. Be sure to stop in front of every illuminated angel to warm each other up with a tight hug and a kiss if you're lucky. Look straight ahead at the biggest Christmas tree in the world and then look down at the famous ice skating rink where friends, families, and lovers race, twirl, and fall. Join them in the fun if you have the time. (*The Rink* at Rockefeller Plaza, 601 Fifth Avenue; 212-332-7654, is open October through April from 8:30 A.M. to 10:00 P.M.) Buy some chocolate to share at Teuscher Chocolatier (620 Fifth Avenue; 212-246-4416) and throw your change into a fountain, both of you closing your eyes and making a wish at the same time. Give each other massages with the massage gadgets at *Brookstone* (620 Fifth Avenue; 212-262-3237). Amble across the street to see the animated displays in the big windows of Saks Fifth Avenue (611 Fifth Avenue, 212-753-4000).

In the summer, the ice skating rink is transformed into a colorful outdoor café with trees and flowers, and tables under pink, green, and tan umbrellas. The restaurants at Rockefeller Center are newly renovated. For information about them, call 212-332-7620.

The annual Rockefeller Center Flower and Garden Show from mid-July until the beginning of August practically turns this already gorgeous complex into a virtual outdoor museum, featuring water lilies and sunflowers, short white picket fences, gazebo-like structures, waterfalls, and finely manicured shrubbery. The imaginative exhibits are created by the region's brightest talents in landscaping and horticultural design. Wander through the gardens together chatting, sipping cappuccino, and admiring the view of the works of art and each other.

Sea Cliff, Long Island

The North Shore of Long Island harbors some of the most charming villages and romantic water views in the New York area. Yet most of the waterfront is private; unless you're pals with a millionaire, beach access is impossible. Accessible beachfront is just one reason, then, to love Sea Cliff. Even though it's in the suburbs, it seems like a small-town movie set. Sea Cliff's secret is its delightful little park on a hill overlooking Long Island Sound. Over the course of a day its charms are many.

From the bench that faces the water, breathe the morning sea air; spend the afternoon chatting. Return in the evening and watch the sun set over the Sound. The park faces northwest, and the sunset can be breathtaking. As you stand on top of a hill away from street lights, you can count the constellations on clear nights.

If you can manage to catch it when it's open, *Once upon a Moose* (304 Sea Cliff Avenue, Sea Cliff, NY 11579; 631-676-9304) is unlike any place you have ever seen. Casual and inexpensive, it's like eating in an eclectic antique gallery. A funky little country place, it serves dinner Wednesday, Thursday, and Friday and lunch between noon and 5:00 P.M. Saturday and Sunday. So sit near the bird cage at one of the little round tables where neither the silverware nor the plates match and have a salad or a sandwich. During the warmer months a few tables are set on the patio for those who like to eat outside.

If southern cuisine is more your taste and you don't mind a noisy crowd, *Tupelo Honey* (inexpensive) is an equally whimsical and unusual restaurant at 39 Roslyn Avenue, Sea Cliff, NY 11579 (631-671-8300). It's a splashy mosaic of deep blue and red tiles, some even on the patio. Big band or Spanish guitar music fills the room and draws a sophisticated crowd. Entreés include roasts, grills, pizzas, and pastas; Tupelo Honey is open every evening for dinner.

If you're traveling in the summer months and would like to explore some of the romantic spots around Sea Cliff, you can start by hiking or driving down the road that winds its way down the cliff to the water below (Cliff Way). This will put you on the boulevard, which quickly becomes Shore Road. A short distance past the bottom of the hill, you will find the entrance to the *Sea Cliff Village Beach*. A small fee is charged for using the white sand beach for swimming or rafting. There is no charge to go to the snack bar on the patio, and from there you can rest on comfortable chairs and enjoy the view of the water.

For those in the mood for a little hike, I highly recommend a drive to the *Garvies Point Preserve* (Barry Drive, Glen Cove, NY 11542; 631-571-8010) a few miles away in Glen Cove. The preserve is open seven days from dawn to dusk. There is also a museum there, which is open every day except Monday from 10:00 A.M. to 4:00 P.M., but although it looked very nice, I've never been inside it. In fact, that may be the very reason the preserve was so enchanting—the lack of a museum crowd. And so, I can't tell you if I'm prejudiced by the fact that we had it all to ourselves, but it was a hot summer Sunday, the museum was closed, and we strolled around the maze of paths, breathing in the perfumed air, following the butterflies' mating dances, and kissing beneath the lush bowers. Take the steep log steps down to the rocky North Shore beach, smell the salt air, see the view of Connecticut not far in the distance, and examine the rocks and shells. Let me know what you think.

Silver Lake Park

ADDRESS: VICTORY BOULEVARD, ONE MILE NORTH OF CLOVE ROAD, STATEN ISLAND

The local Staten Island residents who are regular visitors to Silver Lake Park are going to be mad at me for telling you about this wonderful romantic spot. Located right off Victory Boulevard, hidden from traffic and nestled beside a private golf course and country club, Silver Lake is a pristine reservoir surrounded by grassy hills and trees. On a beautiful summer weekend, you'll see just a few people inline skating, running with their dogs, biking, flying kites, strolling, sunbathing, picnicking, and just plain relaxing. You can, too. The water looks crystal clean and holds healthy numbers of huge bass, but there's no swimming or fishing allowed. Perfect for people who want to get away from the crowd, Silver Lake is a very peaceful place to unwind.

If you get hungry and haven't brought a picnic, you might consider heading south for lunch to the Lake Café on the more popular and populated Clove Lake. This restaurant has the potential to be romantic, but it depends a lot on when you go. In romance and in restaurant selection, good timing is essential. Sometimes the park is noisy with children, the restaurant is crowded with parties, and live local bands play loud oldies music on the patio, but the view of the lake from the expansive windows and patio in summer is very pretty. Delicious barbecue is served outdoors in the summer. Watch children play in the park, ducks play in the water, and people breeze by in their paddleboats and rowboats. Inside the restaurant, which is built like a Swiss ski chalet, the menu is elaborate and kind of expensive — especially for dinner. You can enjoy items such as Boathouse Shrimp, which is described as "grilled shrimp wrapped in bacon and glazed with the chef's homemade barbecue sauce," and surf and turf. Lunch is simpler and more reasonably priced. Another dinner option, if you are in a nostalgic mood and have transportation, is to go to the Parsonage (see page 79).

But for a simple day of fun and play, go find Staten Island's hidden jewel: Silver Lake Park.

*F*rank Sinatra Park, Hoboken, NJ

For a perfect view of the New York skyline, on a rambling walkway that is meant for strolling, holding hands, and kissing under the stars, visit Frank Sinatra Park in Hoboken, New Jersey. Named in honor of the legendary former crooner, Sinatra Park has attracted sweethearts and inline skaters alike, drawing to the clean and safe riverside site a collection of romantics who come to enjoy the view and to take in one of the many musical events that occur in the roundabout from April through the warm-weather season. It's not unusual for the park to host Shakespearean plays, madrigal choirs, jazz and reggae bands, and festivals ranging from the Saint Ann's to craft fairs.

Stop by the on-site *Frank Sinatra Park Café* (inexpensive) at 525 Sinatra Park for an espresso or cappuccino, a glass of wine, or a wide variety of flavored coffees and teas. You can sit at one of the dozen outdoor tables or take your nonalcoholic beverages out to a bench along the walkway for an impromptu picnic overlooking the city that never sleeps. Feed the ducks or just watch the waves rolling up on shore, marvel at the stately schooners floating by, and see if you can't spot the Forbes yacht with its green helicopter perched on top.

Sinatra Park is open to the public at all hours, year-round. You can find it easily by walking along River Street up to Fifth Street; it's on the right-hand side.

Make your evening complete with dinner at nearby Amanda's, one of the most romantic restaurants in Hoboken. In fact, Amanda's was written up by Zagat as a romantic first-date place, and it certainly earned its place in this book with its Victorian charm. Amanda's is a renovated brownstone with an impeccable Italian marble bar, two roaring fireplaces, intricate tapestries and artwork on the walls, hardwood floors, and high-backed chairs. Its romantic ambience is matched only by its extensive menu of delectable appetizers, salads, entreés, and desserts.

The appetizer menu includes sautéed calamari, seared sea scallops, tuna tartare, and the popular mushroom crepe with roasted vegetables. For entreés, they offer black sesame–crusted tuna, pan-roasted red snapper, grilled prime Angus sirloin, roast chicken, and a selection of pastas, other seafood, and various other menu choices. Save room for a shared romantic dessert as well. Take turns feeding each other warm chocolate cake with vanilla ice cream, a banana napoleon, cranberry bread pudding with crème anglaise, or yummy key lime pie. They have an extensive wine list, plus wine specials for those romantic toasts to the two of you, and owners Eugene and Joyce Flynn offer a special early menu from 5:00 to 6:00 P.M. Monday through Saturday, during which their select menu at smaller portions is available.

Reservations are required, dress is casual but neat, and there is a cozy table waiting for you by the fireplace. *Amanda's* (908 Washington Street, Hoboken, NJ 07030, at Washington and Ninth; 201-798-0101) is open Monday through Thursday from 5:00 to 10:00 P.M., Friday and Saturday from 5:00 to 11:00 P.M., and Sunday from 5:00 to 9:00 P.M. They also offer a gourmet brunch from 11:00 A.M. to 3:00 P.M. on Saturday and Sunday, if your preference is for an early romantic get-together.

In view of the immense parking headaches in Hoboken, we suggest taking the PATH from New York City to Hoboken and walking the five easy blocks to Frank Sinatra Park. To reach Amanda's from the PATH station, cross River Street and Hudson Street to get to Washington Street, and then head uptown for nine blocks to their location. If you will be driving from out of the area, parking garages are located on Hudson Street.

Staten Island Ferry and Snug Harbor Cultural Center

ADDRESS FOR STATEN ISLAND FERRY: WHITEHALL STREET AT BATTERY PARK ♥ PHONE: 718-815-2628 (BOAT) ♥ HOURS: 24 HOURS A DAY, SEVEN DAYS A WEEK ♥ ADDRESS FOR SNUG HARBOR CULTURAL CENTER: 1000 RICHMOND TERRACE, STATEN ISLAND, NY 10301 ♥ PHONE: 718-448-2500 ♥ CALL FOR HOURS AND EVENTS. ♥ SNUG HARBOR IS LOCATED TWO MILES WEST OF THE FERRY TERMINAL IN STATEN ISLAND.

Taking the ferry: Even if you never make it to Snug Harbor, don't miss the thrilling experience of an evening sunset "cruise" aboard the Staten Island Ferry. The 5.2-mile ride from Manhattan to Staten Island takes a half hour and it's FREE. Plan to leave early enough to spend the afternoon at Snug Harbor and return while the sun sets, or leave at sunset and take the return ferry back to see the flickering lights of the New York skyline as night descends on the city.

Once on board headed for Staten Island, rush to grab a piece of the railing on the right side of the ferry. If you hadn't just entered through that icky terminal, you would swear you were on the QE2 headed for Europe. Here's where the crush of the crowd works in your favor. Your lover will be forced to wrap around you, rubbing your shoulders maybe, brushing kisses on your cheek. The thundering boom of the foghorn will jolt you even closer together. As you leave the shore, you'll be swaying in each other's arms, feeling the huge engine hum all through you. And the first thing you'll see is one of the most beautiful sights on the planet: the sun setting behind Lady Liberty. While you're on the ferry, she belongs to you. Ships will pass; perhaps you'll see a parasailer or some playful jet skiers—whatever you see, the mood will be one just made for two.

To Snug Harbor: To get to Snug Harbor from the ferry terminal, take the S40 bus. You could walk the two miles, but it isn't very scenic. Snug Harbor cultural center is made up of 28 newly restored historic buildings on 83 bucolic acres of parkland. It was originally built in 1801 as a maritime home and hospital for retired sailors. Now the buildings are used as galleries and workshops and for weddings and cultural activities such as plays, recitals, and art exhibitions. Looking around, you could be anywhere—from New England to the English Highlands.

There is so much about New York City that is nothing like New York City. When was the last time you saw two jet-black swans with bright orange bills swimming in a nearly heart-shaped pond, with a fountain pouring forth rainbows from the center? Stroll through the small botanical garden, within which are many smaller gardens, including the "White Garden," made up of all-white plants and flowers. It will have you dreaming of weddings. But you need not dream for long. Just turn your head and you'll probably see a bride and groom either having their wedding on the premises or stopping to take pictures with their entourage. Nope, not a bad place to have a wedding at all.

The Temple Bar

ADDRESS: 332 LAFAYETTE STREET, NEW YORK, NY 10012 (BETWEEN HOUSTON AND BLEECKER STREETS) ♥ PHONE: 212-925-4242 ♥ HOURS: MONDAY THROUGH THURSDAY 5:00 P.M. TO 1:00 A.M.; FRIDAY AND SATURDAY 5:00 P.M. TO 2:00 A.M.; SUNDAY 7:00 P.M. TO 1:00 A.M. ♥ DRESS: CASUAL ELEGANT ♥ PRICE: EXPENSIVE

Step into the chic Temple Bar on Lafayette Street, and you'll feel as if you've just walked into the exclusive first-class lounge of a 1920s cruise ship. Your entrance into this lush, dark, glamorous establishment takes you past the curled lizard icon on the wall outside, through two doors, and then through a curtain into a mahogany and marble-paneled room that is evocative of something out of *Titanic*, or perhaps the lounge car of the Orient Express.

As a ceiling fan spins lazily overhead, you'll notice the windows hung with red and gold curtains, shutting out all of the sun to create a dark, mystical ambience that is perfect for accenting the European flavors of the rooms. You'll slide onto a black vinyl banquette lit in a perfectly understated way from above by a tiny, thin spotlight that points perfectly to the matches on the table. The slits of light permeate the room, catching the smoky waves at the top of the ceiling and making the brightly colored drinks on your table sparkle.

From this vantage point, you can take in all of the details that have transported you to another place and time: the wall sconces that were salvaged from an authentic 1920s cruise ship; the bar made of Honduran mahogany and nineteenth-century hand-carved Italian oak, with large inlaid panels of green antique Vermont marble; the plush Persian rugs that cover the floors; the low-hung mirrors that make the small attraction seem much larger. All around you are smooth leather chairs occupied by the "beautiful people" of the city, as art magazine editors mix with gallery owners and everyone around you looks like a model. It's the perfect place to see and be seen, as if you had just joined some secret society where the rest of the world ceases to exist.

While it's quiet enough so you can hold hushed conversations with your partner, you'll overhear, past the muted sounds of Sarah Vaughan, romantic jazz, and R&B, the most fascinating conversations. Next to you, a couple may be discussing Roman architecture, a model may be meeting with her agent, a land baron may be plotting her next takeover. They've all come to the sexy Temple Bar to immerse themselves in this escapist world, and you, by being there, have entered their world. It's a romantic adventure, a chance to try out a new identity in a spot that's all about Identity. Your bow-tied bartender may be the next Leonardo DiCaprio, and you can say you knew him when.

You'll hear champagne corks popping, the uncorking of wine bottles, and the unmistakable sound of martinis being shaken to perfection. The Temple Bar is renowned for its martinis, and you might choose to start your foray into its world with a taste of what has made this place famous. The martini here has been called the best in town, and you'll want only the best for your partner and yourself. Indeed, the martinis are intoxicating at first sip, and you'll lose yourself in the smooth flavor. Choose your libations and propose a toast to your partnership, snuggling into that banquette and becoming a part of the bas-relief painting that you have just stepped into.

You'll feel immediately comfortable here, as if you have just found one of the most perfect hangouts on earth, and you'll look great in the flattering lighting. No age lines, no wrinkles. No wonder the beautiful people come here. Light beams are a big fixture in this dark and smart location. Beams are fixed on the artwork, and even the liqueurs get their own spotlight. Indeed, it's the mixture of darkness and light that makes the Temple Bar such a romantic place to visit.

On the menu, you'll find nothing but cold snacks — perfect accompaniments to your martini, cosmopolitan, cognac, sherry, or port. Share with your loved one a half ounce of Beluga caviar, blue point oysters on the half shell, shrimp cocktail, guacamole, and other specialties that are just right for the romantic feeding of one another. While the prices are steep here, and the pretense in your surroundings is high, it's the atmosphere you're paying for. Perhaps it's like a private club, the upper echelon of old society, an elegantly appointed hotel bar of yore, and a step into another world. What could be more romantic?

Top of the Tower at the Beekman Hotel (drinks only)

ADDRESS: 3 MITCHELL PLACE, NEW YORK, NY 10017, CORNER OF EAST 49TH STREET AND FIRST AVENUE ♥ PHONE: 212-355-7300 ♥ HOURS: OPEN SEVEN DAYS 5:00 P.M. TO 1:00 A.M. ♥ PRICE: EXPENSIVE

This is one of the loveliest places in the city. It would be great if you could just drop in for dinner, but the restaurant is often booked for private parties, and unless you're in the mood to just wing it, you better call ahead.

It's truly amazing how inviting and even toy-like the city can appear from this height. The 26th-floor view is not too high, not too low, just right for a glorious panorama: the East River, the Queensboro Bridge, the Roosevelt Island Tramway, the cityscape, and much more. In good weather, take advantage of the open-air balcony—unless your fear of heights tends to set your heart fluttering in the wrong way.

Tables line the windows all around—inside and outside. In good weather, it's fun to sit outside. If you choose to sit inside, where a pianist will play your song for you, of course you'll want to try to get a table by the window. While the restaurant at Top of the Tower is perfectly adequate, we prefer to go there for drinks and light food.

$\mathcal{V}$ince & Eddie's

ADDRESS: 70 WEST 68TH STREET, NEW YORK, NY 10023 (BETWEEN CENTRAL PARK WEST AND COLUMBUS AVENUE) ♥ **PHONE:** 212-721-0068 ♥ **HOURS:** MONDAY 5:00 P.M. TO 11:00 P.M.; TUESDAY THROUGH THURSDAY NOON TO 3:00 P.M. AND 5:00 P.M. TO 11:00 P.M.; FRIDAY NOON TO 3:00 P.M. AND 5:00 P.M. TO MIDNIGHT; SATURDAY 11:00 A.M. TO 3:00 P.M. AND 5:00 P.M. TO MIDNIGHT; SUNDAY 11:00 A.M. TO 3:00 P.M. (BRUNCH) AND 5:00 P.M. TO 11:00 P.M. ♥ **PRICE:** EXPENSIVE

We keep stressing that privacy, so hard to come by in New York, is a crucial romantic catalyst. At Vince & Eddie's the many nooks and crannies and cozy tables for two give you and your date that extra "we're getting away from it all" feeling that enhances your romance. Are we on the Upper West Side on a Tuesday night or is this Thanksgiving Day in Vermont? You'll feel coddled here. The music is classical and unobtrusive. The tables are well spaced for an intimate conversation. And there's a delightful outdoor garden available for seasonable dining.

Home-style but never banal, the meals are solid comfort food with a twist: quails wrapped in bacon with sweet-potato fries; flash-fried calamari with a cilantro citrus dipping sauce. The chef, Scott Campbell, receives high marks from most food critics, and he'll probably emerge from the kitchen at some point to make sure you're happy.

Overall, you'll get a feeling of being well cared for, giving you the peace of mind to concentrate on your romantic partner and the evening's delights ahead.

The combination of décor and comfort food gives you the feel of winter in your country home even in the middle of summer. Here you'll find the enveloping comfort of a bed and breakfast—without the bed, the breakfast, or the four-hour drive. If you're a homespun romantic couple who are weary of New York chic, this may be your perfect Valentine's or Tuesday night destination.

The Water Club

ADDRESS: 500 EAST 30TH STREET, NEW YORK, NY 10016 (AT EAST RIVER) ♥ **PHONE:** 212-683-3333 ♥ **HOURS:** MONDAY THROUGH SATURDAY NOON TO 3:00 P.M. AND 5:00 P.M. TO 11:00 P.M.; SUNDAY 11:00 A.M. TO 3:00 P.M. (BRUNCH) ♥ **DRESS:** JACKETS REQUIRED ♥ **RESERVATIONS** REQUIRED ♥ **PRICE:** EXPENSIVE

Situated on an oversized barge overlooking the East River, the Water Club is an upscale destination designed to impress. While during the summer it does have out-door dining, complete with a dazzling view of the city, the gentle sounds of the water lapping against the shore, and proximity to lazily passing light-strung boats, its indoor ambience is romantic to the fullest.

Thirteen or 14 cozy, well-appointed tables are arranged by the windows for a full view of the skyline, and the flickering candles and gentle spotlights directed on each table give the natural-colored room a warm glow. So as the impressive lights of the city outline the broad horizon outside your window, your eyes will sparkle with the dancing light of the candle between you and your sweetheart. As you look around, you'll see the glowing faces of your fellow diners, each accented by spotlights of their own, making them—and you—the stars of the evening.

As you melt into the atmosphere of the Water Club, you'll hear the quiet tinkling of silverware against plates, the laughter of pleasantly sur-prised guests, and the occasional listing of the dessert offerings, in itself a mood-enhancer. The tone of this restaurant is quiet and classic, cozy and comfortable, allowing you and your sweetheart the ease of your whispered sweet nothings, and no one will mind if you hold hands across the table. While you're at it, no one will notice if the romantic mood of the Water Club has you playing a discreet game of footsie under the table as well.

The sound of champagne corks popping for the various celebrants around the restaurant accents the live piano music—classical and ballads—that accompanies your dining experience. You'll get lost in the music, feeling as if the serenade is for you alone. Feel free to approach the pianist to request "your song," and reminisce about where you were when you first heard that beautiful music together. And as the soloist plays "Some Enchanted Evening," you'll know that you're in the perfect location for all enchanted evenings.

The Water Club features the best in menu offerings, including as appetizers griddled jumbo lump crabcakes, three-cheese ravioli, and house-smoked salmon; the entreés include grilled Atlantic salmon, grilled filet mignon, and Maine lobster. They also offer a raw seafood bar complete with oysters, New England littleneck or cherrystone clams, and beluga and osetra caviar. Share a generous plateful with your partner. As you feed one another, surely you'll realize why such delicacies are considered aphrodisiacs.

Speaking of romantic effects, choose the perfect bottle of wine or champagne from among the award-winning selections on the Water Club's full wine and champagne list. Pop a cork (or pop the question), and propose a romantic toast or two in your fine surroundings.

Yes, the prices are steep here—the best always comes at a price—but there is the option of a prix fixe menu that includes a mixed green salad or minestrone, Atlantic salmon or grilled chicken, side dishes, and a delectable crème brûlée or ice cream selection. With this option, you and your sweetheart don't have to take out a loan to afford a wonderful dining experience in this lovely place. For special occasions, the expense is well worth it. Whether it's your first visit or you're a repeat customer, all patrons are treated like gold here, which is exactly why so many people take the love of their life to the Water Club for occasions such as marriage proposals, anniversary celebrations, and other momentous events. This is not the kind of place that is easily forgotten, and you're sure to remember your special time here for years to come.

If you'd like to avoid the dinner crowd, early risers may choose to visit the Water Club for its Sunday brunch, offering a wide range of dishes from a smoked fish selection to griddled pancakes, roasted meats carved to order, and a variety of desserts. Share the chocolate-dipped strawberries and start your day in a romantic way with the finest that New York has to offer.

$\mathcal{W}$ater's Edge

ADDRESS: 44TH DRIVE AND EAST RIVER ON VERNON BOULEVARD, QUEENS, NY 11101 ♥ **PHONE:** 718-482-0033 ♥ **HOURS:** OPEN SEVEN DAYS NOON TO 3:00 P.M. AND 5:30 P.M. TO 10:00 P.M. ♥ **DRESS:** JACKETS REQUIRED ♥ **RESERVATIONS** RECOMMENDED ♥ **PRICE:** VERY EXPENSIVE

You've seen it featured in *The Mirror Has Two Faces* as the romantic dining backdrop chosen by Barbra Streisand for her movie, and now you experience the same warm, romantic atmosphere at Water's Edge. Begin your journey to this riverfront mecca of fine dining and scenery by taking the restaurant's spectacular free cruise aboard a decorated riverboat from 34th Street and the East River in Manhattan.

Owner Marika Somerstein has brought her European flair to her restaurant. Its attractions are enhanced by dark hardwood floors, handsome antiques, fireplaces, and a comfortable piano bar where a pianist sets the tone for the many celebrations that take place here. Don't be surprised if you witness a marriage proposal or the celebration of a longtime anniversary, as the staff of Water's Edge has put together the perfect setting for the perfect moments. The staff informs us that impromptu slow dancing has taken place near some of the tables—the place is overwhelmingly romantic—so feel free to do the same.

In the summer, seating is arranged outdoors to take advantage of the fine view of the

Manhattan skyline. The restaurant is situated on a pier that offers the perfect setting for pre- or post-dinner strolling. On a warm night, you can walk for hours, or you can stop to hold one another and look out at the cityscape before you.

Zagat's has counted Water's Edge as among the Top 30 dining experiences in the city, which is quite a feat for the restaurant, considering its Queens setting. Further boosting its reputation as one of the city's most romantic places is the fact that concierges from the Plaza, the Pierre, and the Waldorf are constantly referring their clients to this exquisite location for an elegant evening out.

The menu delights, as it comes from the chef who once worked at the Pierre. The selections include appetizers of steamed lobster dumplings, a sage risotto croquette, a trio of smoked fish with sefruga caviar, and duck and wild mushroom strudel. Entreés include poached red snapper, sautéed arctic char, smoked duck breast, and roasted filet of beef. The prix fixe menus are offered at three courses, four courses, and the "Water's Edge Degustation Menu" of five courses. Seafood selections include lobster, shrimp, crab claws, oysters, and clams. Weekend specialties feature a two-and-a-half-pound whole Maine lobster on Friday and aged prime sirloin steak on Saturday. The pastry cart is stocked with delectable baked goods that will please even the most highly trained tastes, so you can end your dining experience with a little taste of heaven.

Water's Edge's extensive wine list annually receives awards from *Wine Spectator* magazine, and all choices are the finest vintage. So order a bottle—or two—and toast your very special bond in a very special setting.

By the time of this book's publication, this highlight spot will have a new addition. A 105-foot yacht decorated like the restaurant will offer the same fine dining experience as Water's Edge, only cruising past some of the finest scenery the city has to offer. Space will be available for 100 to 140 people, and dancing will be a regular event on board.

*W*est 79th Street Boat Basin

WEST 79TH STREET AND THE HUDSON RIVER ♥ CAFÉ PHONE: 212-496-5542

The entire promenade that is sandwiched between Riverside Park and the Hudson River affords a beautiful walk, but the most special stretch is at the 79th Street Boat Basin. Be lulled by the boats languishing at the dock, wave to the boat owners, and if the gate is open, step out onto the pier so you can closely look over the boats while debating which one you would take if given a choice. Behind you, on the promenade, the park is filled with special little touches like the garden designed to attract bees, hummingbirds, and butterflies.

Just beyond the Boat Basin, Riverside Park is an underused oasis of New York. Rent some sturdy bicycles (see the Yellow Pages for a convenient location) and ride north from 72nd Street as far as the spirit moves you and your legs will take you—say, to Grant's Tomb at West 122nd Street, or even as far as the George Washington Bridge. If you're an energetic couple, you may want to ride over the bridge and along the breathtaking Palisades in New Jersey; if you're in a lazy mood, get a picnic from Zabar's (2245 Broadway, New York, NY 10024, at 80th Street; 212-787-2000), bring a blanket and board game, and stretch out under a tree for a while. All seasons bring something special for lovers: see the late autumn foliage; crush your way through the newly fallen winter snow or make some snow angels; smell the flowers in the spring; feel the breeze from the water in the summer.

From May through October, noon through midnight, you can dine at the 79th Street Boat Basin Café, either on real barbecued hot dogs and hamburgers or on reasonably priced gourmet sandwiches and salads. The frequently packed bar specializes in frozen drinks like margaritas and piña coladas. The café overlooks the Boat Basin and the George Washington Bridge. The café's outdoor terrace is an excellent spot for watching the setting sun; since no reservations are taken for parties of two, you can expect at least a 20-minute wait every night at sunset. It's well worth the wait.

Of course, you can choose not to wait at all. Pick up a meal to go, and find your own quiet Shangri-La in Riverside Park.

Index

NOTE: page numbers indicated by **boldface type** refer to
main descriptions of the 52 destinations.

$\mathcal{I}$ndex by Price

RESTAURANTS

About the Author

Sheree Bykofsky is a well-known New York City literary agent and the author and coauthor of numerous books, including *The Best Places to Kiss In and Around New York City* (third edition); *Popping the Question: Real-Life Stories of Marriage Proposals from the Romantic to the Bizarre* (coauthored with Laurie Viera); *Me: Five Years from Now: The Life-Planning Book You Write Yourself*; and *The Complete Idiot's Guide to Getting Published* (coauthored with Jennifer Basye Sander). Sheree lives, works, and loves in New York City.